★ World War I ★

Life in the Trenches

Titles in The American War Library series include:

World War II
Hitler and the Nazis
Kamikazes
Leaders and Generals
Life as a POW
Life of an American Soldier in
  Europe
Strategic Battles in Europe
Strategic Battles in the Pacific
The War at Home
Weapons of War

The Civil War
Leaders of the North and South
Life Among the Soldiers and
  Cavalry
Lincoln and the Abolition of
  Slavery
Strategic Battles
Weapons of War

AMERICAN WAR LIBRARY

★ ★ ★ ★

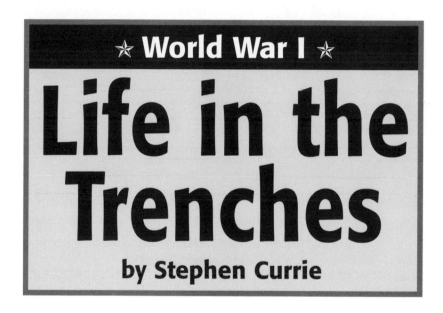

★ World War I ★

Life in the Trenches

by Stephen Currie

Lucent Books, 10911 Technology Place, San Diego, CA 92127

Library of Congress Cataloging-in-Publication Data

Currie, Stephen, 1960–
   Life in the trenches / by Stephen Currie.
      p. cm. — (American war library. World War I)
Summary: Describes the conditions, hardships, and horrors faced
by soldiers in the trenches and on the battlefields of World War I.
Includes bibliographical references (p.   ) and index.
   ISBN 1-56006-838-8
   1. World War, 1914–1918—Juvenile literature. I. Title. II. Series
D522.7 .C87 2002
940.3—dc21

2001004294

Copyright 2002 by Lucent Books, Inc.
10911 Technology Place, San Diego, California 92127

Printed in the U.S.A.

★ Contents ★

A Nation Forged by War

The United States, like many nations, was forged and defined by war. Despite Benjamin Franklin's opinion that "There never was a good war or a bad peace," the United States owes its very existence to the War of Independence, one to which Franklin wholeheartedly subscribed. The country forged by war in 1776 was tempered and made stronger by the Civil War in the 1860s.

The Texas Revolution, the Mexican-American War, and the Spanish-American War expanded the country's borders and gave it overseas possessions. These wars made the United States a world power, but this status came with a price, as the nation became a key but reluctant player in both World War I and World War II.

Each successive war further defined the country's role on the world stage. Following World War II, U.S. foreign policy redefined itself to focus on the role of defender, not only of the freedom of its own citizens, but also of the freedom of people everywhere. During the cold war that followed World War II until the collapse of the Soviet Union, defending the world meant fighting communism. This goal, manifested in the Korean and Vietnam conflicts, proved elusive, and soured the American public on its achievability. As the United States emerged as the world's sole superpower, American foreign policy has been guided less by national interest and more on protecting international human rights. But as involvement in Somalia and Kosovo prove, this goal has been equally elusive.

As a result, the country's view of itself changed. Bolstered by victories in World Wars I and II, Americans first relished the role of protector. But, as war followed war in a seemingly endless procession, Americans began to doubt their leaders, their motives, and themselves. The Vietnam War especially caused people to question the validity of sending its young people to die in places where they were not particularly wanted and for people who did not seem especially grateful.

While the most obvious changes brought about by America's wars have been geopolitical in nature, many other aspects of society have been touched. War often does not bring about change directly, but acts instead like the catalyst in a chemical reaction, accelerating changes already in progress.

Some of these changes have been societal. The role of women in the United States had been slowly changing, but World War II put thousands into the workforce and into uniform. They might have gone back to being housewives after the war, but equality, once experienced, would not be forgotten.

Likewise, wars have accelerated technological change. The necessity for faster airplanes and a more destructive bomb led to the development of jet planes and nuclear energy. Artificial fibers developed for parachutes in the 1940s were used in the clothing of the 1950s.

Lucent Books' American War Library covers key wars in the development of the nation. Each war is covered in several volumes, to allow for more detail, context, and to provide volumes on often neglected subjects, such as the kamikazes of World War II, or weapons used in the Civil War. As with all Lucent Books, notes, annotated bibliographies, and appendixes such as glossaries give students a launching point for further research. In addition, sidebars and archival photographs enhance the text. Together, each volume in The American War Library will aid students in understanding how America's wars have shaped and changed its politics, economics, and society.

Into the Earth

The First World War—or the Great War as it was commonly known at the time—broke out in the summer of 1914. The immediate cause of the war was the assassination of an Austrian archduke by a Serbian nationalist. However, the roots of the conflict lay further back in European history. For many centuries, warfare had been a constant in Europe. National boundaries shifted according to the results of battles, and countries frequently came to one another's aid when attacked. By the late nineteenth century, the wars had become much less prevalent, but the system of alliances continued. By the time of the assassination, the pledges of support among the nations of Europe were as strong as they ever would be, and much of the continent was neatly divided into two opposing camps. Belgium and England were allied in this way, for example; so were Germany and Austria-Hungary. If one of these countries were attacked, the other promised to come to its friend's aid. Moreover, if one declared war against someone else, the ally was expected to follow.

For most of these years, however, the alliances meant little. Austria and France may not have been especially friendly, but they were hardly at war with each other. Even if nations viewed one another with hostility and suspicion, Europe was still a relatively peaceful place. Pledges of support simply did not come into play; there had been no major battles in Central or Western Europe since the Franco-Prussian War, fought between Germany and France in 1871.

When Archduke Ferdinand was killed, however, this system of alliances became very important. Austria-Hungary attacked Serbia, hoping to exact revenge for Ferdinand's death. Without the pledges of support from other nations, this might have been a strictly localized conflict. Because of the alliances, though, the battle quickly spread. Serbia's ally Russia sent troops to help in Serbia's defense. Germany, a friend to Austria-Hungary, entered the conflict on

Most historians consider the assassination of Franz Ferdinand as the event that instigated World War I.

the other side, upholding its part of the bargain it had made years earlier with the Austrians.

As the summer wore on, the conflict grew. What had been a minor incident quickly enveloped nearly every nation in Europe. France joined in on the Serbian side. Germany sent troops through Belgium to attack France. England entered the war in support of Belgium. Turkey helped out its longtime German ally. Before long, Europe was divided. The Central Powers—Germany, Austria-Hungary, Turkey, and several smaller nations—had lined up against the Allies—England, France, Russia, and others. The Great War had begun.

There were confident predictions that the war would be short. The combatants, many reasoned, would soon see the error of fighting. After all, Europe had been at peace during the previous twenty or thirty years. Also, much of Western Europe was now urban and thoroughly industrialized. The wealth of the developed nations depended on peacetime economies. Even if governments were willing to put human lives at stake, none would dare put their economies in the jeopardy of wartime uncertainty.

Moreover, observers argued, military techniques and technology were better than ever. By 1914, new and more powerful weapons made it possible to wipe out entire regiments in much less time than earlier generations of soldiers could have imagined. In addition, mechanized transport and better roads could allow armies to move far more quickly than their counterparts in previous European wars. It was easier to destroy a town, to wound an enemy from a distance, to lay waste to the countryside. Taking all this into account, Kaiser Wilhelm, the emperor of Germany, predicted total victory for his troops by the end of the fall. Many outside Germany believed the Allies would win, but most people had no quarrel with Wilhelm's estimated time frame. It seemed inconceivable that the war would last long, and indeed some early volunteers on both sides were afraid that the fighting would end before they could take part in it.

The Western Front

But, in fact, the war was far from quick. Despite the new technology and know-how, or perhaps in part because of them, neither side seemed to be able to gain an advantage. Instead of speeding forward across the countryside as most strategists had foreseen, the armies had a tendency to find a safe position and remain there. By the end of the fall—Kaiser Wilhelm's projected end of hostilities—the Allies and the Central Powers were hardly moving at all. The war had become, in many areas, a gigantic stalemate.

This was particularly true on the border between France and Germany. Although there were many important battles in countries such as Turkey and Italy, World War I

German emperor Kaiser Wilhelm believed that his troops would obtain a swift and complete victory over the Allies.

was primarily fought along two lines, or fronts. The eastern front ran along the eastern border of Germany and Austria-Hungary; it divided the Central Powers from Russia and Russia's Eastern European allies. The western front, in contrast, stretched through parts of Belgium and France. East of this line was German territory, either land that had been German for generations or land newly won and controlled by Germany. West of the front were soldiers from France and other countries allied with the French.

Throughout the war, the eastern front was relatively changeable. Extremely long and hard to defend, it tended to move one way or the other as the result of battles. The western front, on the other hand, barely moved at all. It quickly became evident that the two sides were well matched along this line. Try as they might, neither side could dislodge the other. Nearly every attempted attack by the Germans ended in failure.

Nearly every Allied attempt to push the Germans back met a similar fate. As the war continued, the battles did not stop. Neither did the death tolls. But until the last few months of the war, when the Allies finally began to push the Germans back, any territory gained or lost on the western front was minuscule indeed.

Evenly matched sides do not guarantee a stalemate in war. Surprise attacks, probing for weak spots in the line, developing new and unexpected weapons—all of these can tip the balance decidedly in one side's favor. Both sides tried to put all these strategies into action, hoping to gain the upper hand. For nearly four full years, however, none of these attempts met with much success. The reason was not hard to find. As the war settled into a struggle in which neither side could seem to carry the day, both Allied and German commanders adopted and perfected an old military strategy: the construction of trenches.

The War to End All Wars

World War I was frequently called the "War to End All Wars." Many people sincerely believed that it would prove to be the last major war ever fought, regardless of its outcome. Some believed that its horrors would inevitably lead to a popular cry for peace, no matter what. Others pinned their hopes on an increasing realization that people everywhere were very much alike. One Allied soldier spoke for many when he wrote of this incident in the neutral zone, quoted in *War Letters of Fallen Englishmen:* "A little German dog trotted up and licked my British face. I pulled his German ears and stroked his German back. He wagged his German tail. My little friend abolished no man's land, and so in time can we."

But others had a more cynical view of the war's probable effect. "It is difficult to believe that the war will heal the nations," wrote another soldier, noting the degree of hatred that drove each side. "Also, I doubt if we shall have such a horror of war as lots of people seem to think. The rising generation won't know what we know, and we shall forget much that is bad. . . . I should not be surprised if, when we are old, we see a repetition of this war." Sadly, the second writer turned out to be correct.

The Trench System

Trenches are, in essence, long ditches dug into the ground, and their defensive value is easy to see. For as long as there have been wars, soldiers have been seeking safety wherever they could find it: keeping low to the ground, hiding behind hills, and searching out fences, walls, large stones, or anything that could offer some protection. In flat, undisturbed country with few artificial barriers, soldiers had often dug themselves shallow holes to lie in during the worst of the fighting. The U.S. Civil War, the Crimean War during the middle of the nineteenth century, and the American Revolution all included digging of this sort.

But World War I raised the art of trench construction to an entirely new level. Whereas in earlier conflicts soldiers had scratched temporary safe harbors out of the ground, World War I saw the careful construction of more or less permanent ditches. Holes in previous wars were hastily made, while World War I trenches could take days, even weeks, to construct.

Earlier trenches had also been small and shallow, only a foot or two deep—just big enough to afford some measure of protection to one or two men who lay on their bellies and pressed their bodies tightly into the

As the war dragged on, soldiers began to construct elaborate trenches designed to last the duration of the war.

soil. In contrast, the trenches on the western front, were massive and elaborate. Deep, wide and most of all long, they represented something entirely new in trench building.

The trenches came into being on the western front late in 1914, after it became clear that Kaiser Wilhelm's prediction of an early victory was incorrect. Pushing forward, for either side, seemed impossible; on the other hand, retreat was unthinkable. The only answer for the military commanders was to keep the armies where they were. Both armies began digging themselves into the relatively flat landscapes of Belgium and France, and soldiers prepared for a long period of waiting. By the summer of 1915, the trench system was securely in place.

Fire Trenches

Trenches varied somewhat in size and shape according to the side that built them and their exact location along the front. According to most accounts, German trenches were slightly better designed, constructed, and maintained than were those of the Allies. Part of this advantage was due to the fact that the Germans had taken most of the best locations for their own trenches. Their earthworks lay on dry ground and often on low hills, while the British and French were forced to build on lower, wetter territory. However, the basic design varied little from trench to trench.

Most often, what soldiers called "the trenches" consisted not of one ditch but several. Nearest the enemy was the so-called fire trench. Because of its closeness to the other side's lines, this trench was the most dangerous place to be. Ideally, the fire trench measured a yard or two back to front, and extended four or five feet into the earth. Sandbags—usually filled with clay or earth rather than sand—would then be piled on the parapet, or the front lip of the trench. This technique raised the effective depth of the trench to eight or even ten feet. The thickness of the sandbags also provided some extra protection for soldiers. In some areas, however, troops were unable to dig more than a foot or so into the ground before running into water. In those cases, the height of the pile of sandbags had to be increased accordingly.

Although the fire trench was occasionally built in one long, straight line, commanders tried to avoid this type of construction when they could do so. Straight trenches were easy enough to dig, but they presented one major drawback: If an enemy were to reach a perfectly straight trench, a single burst of machine-gun fire could sweep throughout the entire section, killing and wounding everyone in sight.

To avoid this possibility, British and German soldiers usually dug trenches in a crenellated shape, much like the top of a castle wall, and French soldiers opted for a zigzag pattern. The unbroken straight sections, rarely more than ten yards long, were known as firebays. The soldiers spent most of their time in this part of the fire trench. The twists and turns, which served as breaks in the line, were called traverses.

If soldiers were lucky, the soil into which they burrowed was thick and dry. That combination was rare, however. More often, the dirt crumbled easily or turned almost instantly to mud, leading to cave-ins. As a result, the sides of the trench were usually reinforced with sandbags, wood, or wire. Even so, frequent maintenance was needed to keep the sides from falling.

The bottom of the fire trench was also reinforced to keep it from washing away completely during rainstorms. Most often, soldiers put down lengths of wood called duckboards. These were essentially wooden ladders with thick rungs. They allowed water to drain while still—in theory at least—providing the men with solid footing. Because the ideal depth of the trenches was eight or ten feet, fire trenches included a special step in the front. This step allowed soldiers to see and fire their guns over the edge of the parapet.

Saps, Secondary Trenches, and Barbed Wire

Extending forward from the fire trenches were small trenches known as saps. In most areas, these saps were much narrower than a standard trench, barely wide enough for one man to walk alone. They stuck out as far toward enemy lines as commanders dared build them; in some cases, they jutted another thirty or forty yards past the fire trench itself. At the end of the saps were listening posts, where sentries were placed. From such close quarters, sometimes it was possible for these soldiers to see and hear information that would prove valuable.

The fire trenches and the saps were only the front section of the trench system. Behind the fire trenches were one, two, and sometimes as many as ten other lines of trenches, each cut more or less parallel to the fire trench. Known as travel, reserve, or support trenches, these ditches were essential to the war effort. Like the fire trench, these trenches were cut in zigzag or crenellated patterns. Indeed, these secondary trenches looked much like the fire trench, although since they could be constructed a

---

Cans and Wires

In *Memoirs of War, 1914–15*, French soldier Marc Bloch describes the methods his company used to protect their trenches.

To protect the front of our trenches and to set up obstacles in the gaps between them, we were given wire. . . . I assigned two men to string the wire. The task was not without danger, and they were not happy to have been chosen. Yet afterward they felt decidedly proud of themselves and very ready to recall the episode. In any case, they did their best. I accompanied them with loaded rifle in hand, ready to shoot if by chance we met a German at a turn in the woods. I also remember fastening strands of wire around some empty cans that I placed on the ground in front of us, hoping they might trip any advancing enemies and betray them by the noise. What unnecessary anxiety those wretched cans would cause us later! The wind, or a branch falling from a nearby tree, would cause them to clatter from time to time, and clenching our rifles, we would exclaim: "The enemy!"

This aerial photograph shows how complex and intricate the trench system could be. World War I trenches could take weeks to construct, and there could be as many as eleven trenches lined up together.

bit farther from the front line, they were often somewhat bigger and more comfortable.

As their names suggest, the reserve and support trenches were designed to help and encourage the men in the fire trench. Farther back from the fighting and therefore safer, they usually housed the medical staff, kitchens, senior officers, soldiers waiting to be summoned to the front line, and a variety of weapons. These trenches were linked to one another and to the fire trench via narrow communications trenches, usually dug in a zigzag formation just as the main trenches were.

The final feature of the trenches was barbed wire. The distance between the German lines and those of the Allies varied considerably along the western front. At some points, the two sides were nearly a mile apart. At most other locations, however, the fire trenches were much closer; often, the gap between them was only two hundred yards, and occasionally it was a good deal less even than that. In between the German and Allied trenches was a section of ground called no-man's-land, a neutral zone belonging to neither side. To provide extra protection, both armies set up massive barriers of barbed wire as far into no-man's-land as they dared. On the German side, wire often stretched from the fire trench a distance of a hundred feet into the neutral zone, and the French and British were not far behind.

Aerial photographs of the time show clearly the complexity of the trench system. Pictures snapped by pilots reveal a network of lines spreading across the horizon like a spiderweb. Men who flew across the western front marveled at the intricate designs formed by the trenches on both sides. "For the first time I saw the front line as it really was," remarked British pilot Billy Bishop upon viewing the trenches from six hundred feet up. "Now running straight, now turning this way or that in an apparently haphazard and unnecessary curve."[1]

Indeed, the trenches were nothing if not extensive. By some estimates, at the end of 1915 there were twenty miles of trench for each mile of front, and the number of trenches only increased with time. The construction of a trench took thousands of man-hours; maintenance took even more. Demand for shovels and spades soared, and army leaders spent enormous sums of money on wood, wire, and other supplies to construct and keep up the trenches. Yet, in the end, they had little choice. By the end of 1914, it was clear that the war would not soon be over, and it was even more clear that the story of the war would be the story of the trenches.

Chapter 1

Fighting

Few of the men who arrived in the trenches were prepared for the experiences they would face. Many, probably most, had never fought in a war. As for those who had previously served, nearly all had fought a very different kind of war. These men had little or no experience with trench warfare, and for good reason: No one, anywhere in the world, had ever fought such an extensive trench war before.

New recruits on both sides were transported to the front lines by train or bus, a ride most would just as soon have skipped altogether. The transports were crowded and moved with astonishing slowness. Battle units traveled together, and these units could include thousands of men. The logistics of getting all these soldiers on board and sending them in the right direction were nearly insurmountable.

Once near the front lines, the men walked to the trenches. These marches were grueling. Typically, men walked for fifty minutes, often at a frenzied pace, and then rested for ten. Soldiers marched according to this schedule regardless of the weather, and they usually carried at least fifty pounds' worth of gear on their backs. Men frequently fainted or simply could not go on. Those who lasted reached the rearmost trench and prepared to move forward and take their places in the front line.

This final stage of the journey was perhaps the most difficult of all. Because of the possibility of enemy attack, it was necessary to make this march under the cover of darkness. Men moved slowly through the communications trenches, often getting lost, tripping over sleeping soldiers, and stumbling into the walls. If the bottom of the trench was covered in water or solid mud, as it often was in wet weather, the going was even more difficult.

For most soldiers, the experience was frightening, exhausting, and perhaps even worse so near the end of the journey. "When at last we came into the deep communication trench we felt that the end of weariness

One of the most grueling activities that World War I soldiers had to endure was the frenzied march to the front line. Soldiers often carried over fifty pounds on their backs, and they usually marched for fifty-minute-stretches before resting.

must surely be near," wrote British infantryman A. P. Herbert. Unfortunately, he continued, he was wrong. "It was a two-mile trudge in the narrow ditches to the front line," he mourned. "This is the kind of thing, more than battle or blood[,] which harasses the spirit of the infantryman and composes his life."[2] Many other recruits arriving in the fire trench for the first time would echo his sentiment.

Changes in Strategy

Once inside the trenches, life for the soldiers revolved around fighting. Just because the two sides were more or less evenly matched did not mean that the war came to a quick end. If anything, the fighting was prolonged. Despite the balance between the Allies and the Central Powers, fighting continued as each side tried to gain an upper hand. Both sides fired guns and bombs into the other one's lines in a vain attempt to dislodge or at least frighten the enemy. And soldiers often dashed through no-man's-land toward the opposite trenches, hoping to capture men, matériel, or even territory. Some of these attacks were successful. Most, however, only wasted ammunition and human lives.

There were a few stretches along the front where fighting was sporadic. After a major battle in 1915, the stretch of the front near Festubert, France, was largely calm for the rest of the war. One historian described the British trenches in that part of the line as "like a drawing-room with grenade boxes in pyramids . . . and men everywhere dusting and polishing like housemaids."[3] In areas such as this one, it was almost possible to forget, at least temporarily, that the two sides were at war.

But along most of the western front, to forget about the war would have been impossible. The sound of gunfire was ever present. Soldiers slept, ate, and lived with their weapons always at the ready. At any moment there could be a raid from the opposing trenches, a dozen or more enemy soldiers dropping unexpectedly onto the duckboards. At any moment, too, an artillery shell could explode several yards behind a soldier's head—or on the spot where he was standing. Or there could suddenly come the signal to go "over the top"—to climb over the parapet that formed the front wall of the fire trench and head into the danger of no-man's-land.

The trenches, then, did not replace or prevent fighting; they simply altered it. In previous wars, most combat was at close range, often hand-to-hand. Fighters stood across a battlefield from one another, charging and retreating as necessary and using swords, knives, or guns to attack or defend themselves. This style of fighting was known as waging a war of movement. By putting soldiers in fixed positions and hiding them away, the trench system made it virtually impossible to fight that sort of a war. Although military commanders were slow in recognizing that the trenches had made wars of movement obsolete, they gradually began to change their tactics.

Offense and Defense

The most important value provided by the trenches was defensive: They provided an artificial barrier that helped halt enemy progress. Digging in made it difficult for another army to pass. The barbed wire, the sandbags, and the zigzag shape of the various trenches all blocked easy access into the opposition's territory. In previous wars, it was impossible to predict where fighting might take place, and communities many miles from the scene of one battle could easily be the site of the next. During World War I, in contrast, towns safely behind the last of the supply trenches could expect to see very little fighting.

The trenches also served a defensive purpose by shielding troops from danger. On one level, the protection afforded by the trenches was real. A soldier who stood behind a thick pile of sandbags could indeed guarantee that he would not be hit by a bullet from an opposing gun. Similarly, a recruit who lay flat on the ground of his trench had little to fear from shrapnel, the metal projectiles sent whizzing in all directions by exploding bombs.

Yet the trenches also presented a serious safety problem for the men who lived in them. Although they protected soldiers from certain kinds of danger, they could also serve as a death trap. The trench system crowded men into small and predictable areas. Thus, an officer who could locate the opposition's fire trench—usually an easy enough task—automatically knew where most of the opposition soldiers would be. And escaping from the trenches during an emergency was a difficult job. The high walls, the thick layers of sandbags, the parapet, and the narrow communication channels all were designed to keep the enemy out; they were nearly as successful at keeping the other side in. Soldiers in a trench could be trapped and killed in a way that could never take place on an open battlefield.

There was little rest in the trenches due to the constant nature of the fighting; soldiers had to keep their weapons close by even when sleeping and eating.

Communication

Telephone systems changed communication in the trenches; the front line could send and receive messages with the other trenches.

The invention of the telegraph and the telephone in the nineteenth century changed warfare as well as the world in general. Before these devices, it was difficult to transmit messages beyond the range of the speaking voice. Soldiers and officers worked out various signaling systems using flags and telescopes or binoculars, but these were inefficient, open to misinterpretation, and easily intercepted by the enemy.

World War I still relied on some of these old systems, but communication was done through wire whenever possible. The trenches were equipped with telephones connected by a network of wires stretching across the entire system. That way, officers at the rear could speak directly with men at the front, as well as with machine gunners and other artillerymen elsewhere on the battlefield. The most up-to-date information could be passed along quickly and easily, so commanders could make snap decisions about tactics based on the situation at hand.

The telephone system had several important drawbacks. Wires were hard to maintain. Connections were sometimes knocked out, and the quality of reception was usually poor. Worse, enemy soldiers sometimes managed to tap into the other side's wiring, enabling them to listen in on all conversations. But even though this sort of communication was far from perfect, World War I did represent the beginning of a new age in warfare—an age in which distant communication was a given from the start.

Consequently, both armies soon realized that the trenches could be used for offensive purposes as well as for defense. For the most part, this meant attacking from the safety of one's own lines. Where the fire trenches were close enough, for instance, soldiers often used hand grenades to harass the opposition. From a short distance, a man with a strong and reasonably accurate arm could lob a grenade into the enemy's fire trench. Even if it did not kill anyone when it exploded, the grenade still had a good chance of inflicting wounds, blowing holes in sandbags, or damaging supplies. Perhaps more important, hand grenades helped keep the opposition nervous and off balance.

Early in the war, grenades were not nearly as standardized a weapon as they later became. Almost any material could be used to create a small explosive, and almost any material were. The Germans developed a grenade known to English soldiers as the "potato masher"; it consisted of a five-inch-long handle, a nine-inch cylinder, and streamers at the end to improve its flight. As for the British, one of their earliest attempts to fashion a productive grenade began with a jam jar (or jam-pot), and then followed this procedure: "Take a jam-pot, fill it with

To harass the enemy and throw them off balance, soldiers on both sides made small explosives called hand grenades.

shredded gin cotton and ten penny nails, mixed according to taste. Insert a No. 8 detonator and a short length of Bickford's Fuse. Clamp up the lid. Light with a match. . . and throw for all you are worth."[4]

Snipers and Sharpshooters

Another useful offensive weapon in trench warfare was the rifle. The most complicated of these had telescopic sights, but any rifle would do as long as it could shoot reasonably accurately. Those who fired the rifles were called snipers. Some of these men stayed within the trenches. They stood on the step below the parapet, hoisted their rifles over the top, and fired off as many shots as they dared before ducking back into the relative safety of the trench. Often, soldiers constructed special metal loopholes at the

Soldiers serving as snipers had the difficult task of finding an effective place to shoot from. To make this task easier, snipers often tried to lure out the enemy by using trickery.

top of the parapet. The idea of these holes was to make sighting easier by keeping the rifle steady. The most experienced sharpshooters, however, disdained their use: Not only could they aim well enough without it, but they realized that their loopholes were a tempting target for opposing snipers.

Not all snipers stayed within the trenches. Most found other places from which to fire. Some climbed out into the saps and ventured as far into no-man's-land as they dared. Under the right circumstances, that could be quite a long way. "Off I crawled through sodden clay and trenches, going about a yard a minute," wrote one British sniper. "I crawled . . . very slowly to the parapet of their trench." There was a German nearby, he reported; "I saw his teeth glistening against my foresight [of the rifle], and I pulled the trigger very slowly. He just grunted, and crumpled up."[5]

Other snipers went along the lines till they found a rock, a tree, or some other feature that would enable them to shoot from higher up. In a few cases, soldiers built hollow trees or other artificial structures that could be placed where the shooter could do the most damage. However, most snipers chose not to stay in one position for so long. As a rule, it was safer to move around. Movement not only made it harder for the sniper to be found, but also made the direction of the next shot less predictable.

Sniping was a difficult business. For the most part, a soldier who stayed down at the bottom of the trench was safe enough from this kind of gunfire. The angle of the shot meant that men had to be more or less even with the parapet before they could be hit. As a result, it was necessary to get men to look up over the parapets to have a chance to shoot them. Both sides often resorted to trickery to encourage the enemy to look up. One favorite German tactic was to fly a kite with English words on it, hoping the British soldiers in the opposite trench would forget their concern for safety and crane their necks upward to read the message. Often enough, the ruse worked.

Unfortunately for those who lived in the trenches, any man who failed to keep his head down stood a decent chance of being wounded or killed. That was true even when men did not present themselves as a target for long. Although it was difficult to hit a moving target, some sharpshooters, like the German Walter Schmidt, became well known for their abilities to fire quickly and with deadly accuracy. These top marksmen studied the layout of the trenches carefully. Not only were they quick on the trigger, they also knew where the enemy's most vulnerable areas were, and they made excellent use of this information. One British officer, sticking his head up for only a second, was struck by not one but two different sniper bullets from the German side.

Most of the men who were hit with rifle fire were only wounded by it, but sniping could be deadly. In fact, the death toll from sniper fire was surprisingly high given how hard it was to shoot under the circumstances of trench warfare. "Sergeant Doherty was killed by a sniper while supervising a building fatigue," wrote one English officer in 1915. "This is the eighteenth casualty . . . we have lost in this way since we came into the line on Tuesday."[6]

Another useful weapon for trench warfare was the machine gun. Mounted on tripods and kept back from the frontmost line, the machine guns were large, bulky, and expensive. Still, they were truly terrifying weapons when turned against an opposing trench. The machine guns could do more than kill men; they were also used to

chip away at the enemy's parapets. Every hit by machine-gun fire carried away a little more of the protection supplied by the sandbags, further exposing the soldiers in the trench. "I know nothing more depressing in the midst of battle," wrote a French soldier, "than the steady tac-tac-tac of that deadly weapon."[7]

During World War I, the machine gun proved an effective weapon. Many machine guns, such as the one pictured below, utilized a water jacket surrounding the barrel to keep it cool and to prevent it from warping.

Shells

Perhaps the most effective weapons for use against the opposing trenches were not bullets, however, but shells—large projectiles fired by cannon-sized artillery pieces placed in the supply trenches or elsewhere behind the front lines. Shells could be enormous. One German shell, the size and shape of a large bucket, contained two hundred pounds of a thick moist paste to give it extra bulk. Some Allied shells were even larger.

Once launched from a heavy gun, these shells traveled up to seventeen hundred miles per hour and had a range of several miles. "They are the most ghastly things imaginable," reported an English soldier in a letter to his parents, describing the firing of several very large shells. "When they exploded they shook all the ground right round here—and they make a hole 30 ft. deep and 50 ft. across."[8] Even smaller shells were nearly as effective at killing soldiers and blasting holes in the opposition's trenches.

The static nature of the conflict made artillery easy to use along the western front. The guns that shot the shells were bulky and hard to maneuver, especially through mud, ice, and hilly terrain. In a war of movement, their impact would have been lessened; it would have been impossible to bring the guns into position quickly enough to be of help in most battles. During the Great War, however, the situation was different. The trench system meant that troops stayed in one position for months, even years. Under these conditions, it made perfect sense to take the time to bring the cannons into position and let them shoot.

As a result, artillery shells were possibly the single most important weapon in the fight along the western front. Although on some days relatively few shells would be fired—perhaps only five or six by each side—long and sustained bombardments were more usual. The statistics regarding artillery use are staggering. On one day in September 1917 alone, the British fired off nearly a million rounds of ammunition from their heavy guns. A two-week period of heavy fire outside Ypres, Belgium, cost the British another 4 million rounds or more. In strategically sensitive areas, most soldiers agreed, the sound of shells going off was constant. As a British soldier put it,

> The sound was different, not only in magnitude but in quality, from anything known to me. It was not a succession of explosions or a continuous roar; I, at least, never heard either a gun or a bursting shell. It was not a noise, it was a symphony . . . a condition in the atmosphere, not the creation of man.[9]

For the men in the trenches, there was little protection against the power of the shells. These projectiles were deadly and usually unstoppable. If a well-aimed shell exploded as it fell into the middle of a trench, anyone in close range would be killed or maimed. Lying prone on the duckboard floor, hiding in the dugouts, burrowing into sandbags—all were useless against the

Gunners remove an empty shell casing. Shells proved to be the most effective weapon in trench warfare; they could travel up to seventeen hundred miles per hour and could make a hole thirty feet deep and fifty feet across.

strength of a shell. "Men were ordered to take cover in the tunnels, but of what avail?" reported an Australian soldier who barely survived an exceptionally fierce enemy shelling. "A shell would come crashing through the tunnel and bury unknown numbers alive."[10] At least two hundred Allied soldiers were killed during that particular bombardment, and the scene was repeated in dozens of other stretches of the line along all fronts.

Fortunately for the men in the trenches, shells often failed to inflict all the damage they could have caused. One reason was that many of the shells never exploded. In the language of the troops, they were duds. Another problem was lack of accuracy. Al-though the range of the heaviest guns could be as much as six miles, it was simply not possible to locate a target and be sure of hitting it. There were too many unknowns: exactly how far off the intended target lay, precisely how high to shoot the projectile, the effect of weather, and the amount of gunpowder that would help send the shell on its way.

The answers to some of these questions could be computed using mathematics, but during a steady bombardment there was no time, and gunners had to rely on their best instincts. Sometimes their estimates were far off, and shells crashed more or less harmlessly in no-man's-land or soared far over the rearmost trenches. Occasionally, attempts to lob shells into the enemy's front lines would fall so short that the shell would explode before reaching no-man's-land. This so-called friendly fire cost many lives throughout the war.

Gas

Besides artillery, World War I saw the introduction of one other extremely dangerous weapon: poison gas. By releasing a cloud of toxic gases, one side could either force the enemy out of its trenches or kill off those who stayed. Tear gas was introduced into the war as early as January 1915. The Germans introduced the much more lethal chlorine gas the following April, and before long both sides were making frequent use of various deadly chemicals.

These chemicals were surely the most appalling weapon in use during the war. A cloud of gas rolling in on the wind was essentially unstoppable. Ducking down into

Tear gas and chlorine gas, which stayed close to the ground, were frequently used in World War I to force the enemy out of its trenches.

To protect against poison-gas bombs, soldiers either tied a wet handkerchief around their mouth and nose, or wore gas masks that filtered out the dangerous chemicals. Although the masks were uncomfortable, they prevented a great deal of damage to the soldiers' lungs and skin.

the trenches was of no help: The clouds of deadly gas tended to stay low to the ground, so the concentration of fumes was actually worse the lower a soldier tried to go. The poison had dramatic effects. "Their lungs are gone," wrote one hospital worker of men who had been gassed, "literally burnt out. Some have their eyes and faces entirely eaten away by gas and their bodies covered with first-degree burns."[11] The injuries were often only temporary, but many men died, and others, once gassed, never truly recovered.

Even if the effects of the gas did not linger, the experience itself was horrifying. "With the cloud, death enveloped us," wrote a French soldier who had been in the trenches when the Germans launched a gas attack. "We had seen everything . . . but nothing [could] compare with this fog which for hours that felt like centuries hid from our eyes the sunlight, the daylight, the clear whiteness of the snow."[12] In comparison, the prospect of being hit with a shell seemed downright pleasant. As a result, fear of being gassed was a constant in trench life.

Like shells, poison gases were imperfect as weapons. Perhaps the biggest problem was that the weather did not always cooperate. "I asked him how he arranged to have a favorable wind,"[13] a British general wryly remarked when a subordinate suggested using chemicals early in 1915. His point was well taken: If the breeze shifted suddenly, the gases would roll back onto the attacker's own army. Wet weather likewise could interfere with the effectiveness of the compounds.

As time went on, armies developed protections against the chemicals. For some, a wet handkerchief tied around the mouth and nose could counteract most of the ill effects. For others, army specialists designed gas masks, helmets, and other preventative measures which provided men with a small but steady supply of pure air. These masks did not eliminate the danger of gas attacks, but they did save many men from horrible deaths. Unfortunately, they were also uncomfortable. "We gaze at one another like goggle-eyed, imbecile frogs," complained one English soldier. "The mask makes you feel only half a man."[14] Still, feeling like an imbecile frog was preferable to dying from blistered, burned-out lungs.

Raids

Attacking the enemy did not always mean launching shells or clouds of gas from a safe distance away. Both sides engaged in frequent raids of various kinds on the other army's trenches. Ideally, a raid would take the enemy by surprise. Caught off guard by the sudden arrival of a number of opposition soldiers, the army would surrender, leaving soldiers, trenches, and weapons in the hands of the invaders.

Prisoners

The odds of being taken prisoner during World War I were rather high. Because the opposing trenches were so close, any misstep could result in capture. A raid that went wrong, a soldier lost in no-man's-land, a sleeping sentry—all of these situations could result in men being taken prisoner.

Half a million French soldiers were captured by the Germans during the conflict. The Allies captured substantial numbers of German soldiers, too. But these prisoners were typically not kept near the front for long. Instead, they were shipped behind the lines to prison camps. Some of the prisoners did hard labor on farms or in factories while imprisoned; most, however, were given little or nothing to do. Thus, the prison camps were usually experiences in intense boredom.

Approximately one prisoner in eleven did not survive the experience. Unsanitary conditions in the camps played a big role in the high death rate. So did poor nutrition, overcrowding, and exposure to the elements. And of course many soldiers were already in a weakened condition from their stints in the trenches. For the most part, however, soldiers did not die because of deliberate mistreatment. On both sides, the numbers of prisoners turned out to be more than the logistics could handle.

nally, raids could be a bonding experience. Army divisions competed to see who could carry out the most effective raids, and the ties between men who survived the experience were certainly strengthened as a result of it.

Even if soldiers made it through most of no-man's-land during an attack, they often encountered difficulty when trying to get through the defensive barbed wire.

Over the Top

But raids paled in comparison to full-blown attacks. From time to time, one of the armies would launch an offensive in which hundreds of soldiers would spring over the parapets and make their way toward the other trenches. The purpose of these attacks was not the small-scale victory of the successful raid. Instead of taking a few prisoners, shooting a few enemy soldiers, and finding out a few bits of information about the other side's plans, these attacks attempted to drive the enemy out of the trenches altogether.

While the raids occasionally took on a kind of party atmosphere, the full-scale attacks were deadly serious. Preparations for these attacks usually began some days in advance. Veteran soldiers always knew the signs. One was the sudden extra concern among officers that every man have the necessary equipment, including an effort to replace worn out weapons. Another was the distribution of identity disks, or dog tags that revealed the man's name and rank. A third, sometimes, was more food. "The old hands judged all the signs correctly," reported a journalist who spent time in the trenches, "and summed them up in a sentence, 'Being fattened for the slaughter.'"[17]

At a prearranged signal, usually given at dawn, men all along the front line of a fire trench would "go over the top," or scale the parapet. The attacks could involve dozens of men or thousands. During the Battle of the Somme, for instance, an unbroken line of British soldiers sixteen miles long swarmed out of the trenches at the same moment. The soldiers were armed with similar implements to those the men carried on their raids: grenades, rifles, and extra ammunition. Ten minutes before scaling the parapets, an officer would double-check that all was prepared.

The signal to move forward was usually simple enough: the sound of a shrill whistle, the fall of a cap. At the same time, the artillery, toward the rear, would begin to fire frantically toward no-man's-land; the purpose was to clear the space in front of the onrushing troops and to make shooting at them harder. Usually, the men were stretched out so that there was a space of a yard or two between each pair. Once the first group of soldiers had traveled some twenty yards, a second wave of troops spilled over the top and out into the neutral area.

The theory behind the attack was that moving in unison would frighten and unnerve the enemy. Consequently, officers did their best to keep their troops in order. "My old colonel walked in front of our ragged line and gave the signals by a wave of his cane,"[18] reported one soldier. Commanders also believed it would not be possible for the enemy to shoot all the attackers if they traveled quickly enough and were sufficiently well armed.

But the commanders who held this belief were wrong. Under the circumstances of trench warfare, to launch a full-scale attack generally meant to commit suicide, and the soldiers—if not the generals—knew it. The casualties from these battles were appalling. The British Tenth Brigade had twenty-four hundred officers and soldiers killed trying to cross no-man's-land in one battle; that amounted to almost the entire troop. In another fight, a second British battalion lost so many men that only fifty soldiers made it unscathed to the German lines.

Even the divisions which were not totally annihilated frequently lost half or more of their men to injury or death. "I see rows upon rows of British soldiers lying dead, dying or wounded in No Man's Land," a British eyewitness wrote after one such attack. "The men fell in their ranks, mostly before the first hundred yards of No Man's Land had been crossed."[19] Some attackers did get closer; most, however, did not.

The problem was twofold. One issue was that the trenches were too well defended. In order to get over the parapets and into neutral territory, soldiers had to remove sandbags and cut their own barbed wire; both provided a tipoff to the enemy that an attack was imminent. The opposing trenches themselves, of course, were also blocked with wire and other obstacles, and the trek through no-man's-land to reach the enemy trenches was usually very difficult because of the craters from shells that had missed their targets.

The more serious problem, though, was the effectiveness of the weapons available to the defenders. With their machine guns and accurate rifles, the crowds of men picking their way through the neutral zone had little chance to avoid being shot. "There could never before in war have been a more perfect target than this solid wall of khaki men," reported a German regimental historian about a British attack. "There was only one possible order to give: 'Fire until the barrels burst.'"[20] Another German machine gunner remarked that aiming was unnecessary:

There were so many soldiers that firing randomly worked just as well.

Successful Attacks

Once in a while, to be sure, an onrushing attack would succeed. A machine gun would jam, a defending brigade would panic, or artillery fire would drive back much of the opposition, so at least some significant share of the soldiers who started out would reach the enemy trenches. Upon reaching the fire trench, the attackers typically swung down over the parapets and rocked the trenches and dugouts with gunfire and grenades, sweeping them free of enemy soldiers.

Often, however, the gunfire was unnecessary, because the men still trapped in the trenches surrendered first. Sometimes the attackers were merciful; sometimes they were not. "Lying on his stomach," said one English soldier about a German captive, "he turned his head and asked for mercy but his eyes said murder. I plunged my bayonet into the back of his heart and he slumped with a grunt."[21] Those who were taken prisoner were brought back to the other lines and put in a military lockup.

Taking a trench was cause for celebration, but typically even this was a hollow victory. For one thing, it was rare to advance much more than a trench at a time. Even if the attackers managed to gain control of the other side's fire trench, the remaining soldiers merely retreated into the first of the support trenches and closed off the communication trenches leading forward.

Little had been settled: There was now only a slightly shifted no-man's-land and a front that had moved a hundred yards or so.

Worse, even the most successful attacks always suffered dreadful losses. The joy of the survivors was tempered by the knowledge that many of their friends and comrades had been killed or maimed in the effort. Their joy was tempered, too, by the knowledge that they could easily have been victims as well. The appearance of victory, even here, was too often only an illusion. Fighting was a given for the men who lived in the trenches. That was hard enough to cope with, but what made it far worse was the sheer wastefulness of the fight.

Chapter 2

Duties and Discipline

The moment a soldier arrived in the trench system, he was assigned certain duties to carry out. For the most part, these duties did not vary much from one day to the next. Most were routine, many were dangerous, some were mind-numbing, but all were important. That is generally true in wartime, but it was especially true of the men in the trenches during the First World War. When the enemy was only a football field or two away, the consequences of failing to perform necessary responsibilities could mean death.

Not all soldiers shared precisely the same daily routine. What one man did might match exactly the responsibilities of a fellow soldier several yards or miles down the line. But sometimes the duties did not match as much as complement one another. Commanders made use of specialists and generalists alike. The overarching goal was threefold: to keep the trenches in top condition, to every extent possible; to build up strong defenses against the opposing army; and to prepare for a possible attack against the enemy. As a result, most of the jobs helped support at least one of these goals—and sometimes all three.

Rotation and Relief

Contrary to popular opinion today, World War I soldiers did not spend all their time living in the trenches. The sheer number of troops, if nothing else, dictated that not all soldiers on both sides could fit inside the system. With hundreds of thousands of available men on both sides, even a front several hundred miles was not long enough to contain all the troops. Moreover, it was a long-standing military tactic to hold back at least some men for support and relief purposes. As the war dragged on, it became clear that the unique conditions of trench warfare required a relatively quick rotation of troops. The constant threat of shells, gas, and other dangers dulled men's minds and reflexes and led to despair; many of those who stayed in the trenches for long soon lost their fighting edge and became more or less useless.

As a result, both the Allies and the Central Powers quickly developed ways of rotating men in and out of the front lines. Early in the war, before it was apparent that the fighting had become a battle of the trenches, whole battalions might stay in the front lines for weeks. By the middle of 1915, though, it was rare for a fighting unit to spend more than a few days in the fire trenches. The rest of the time, those men would be stationed in the rear trenches or resting away from the trench system altogether.

The exact amount of time spent in each place varied considerably, according to the needs of the army at the time. By 1915, for

Fighting conditions occasionally required soldiers to remain in their frontline trenches for weeks at a time.

instance, German soldiers near Kemmel Hill typically rotated on a strict ten-day system: four days in the fire trenches, two under less grueling circumstances in the support trenches, and finally four days spent resting. Allied soldiers at the Somme the following winter followed a thirty-two-day schedule: Their units spent eight days at the front, eight in reserve, eight more at the front and eight at rest. Of course, sometimes the circumstances of the battle required minor changes in their routine.

But in most other cases, routine had to be thrown completely out the window. "I am still stuck in this trench," wrote one English soldier to his sister, "and so far as I know not likely to be relieved for some days, as I've had a week of it, and the regulation dose is four days." [22] An exceptionally heavy series of losses by one side in a certain section of the line would often require another regiment to spend extra time at the front. A large-scale planned attack might force commanders to bring in other battalions from their scheduled rest periods. Or—as perhaps happened to the English soldier quoted above—an attack by the enemy on another place in the line might divert relief troops from their scheduled duties.

Whatever the reason, many men had no real idea of when they would be arriving in the trenches—and once there, how long they would stay. One English battalion spent fifty-one consecutive days in the front line. An English officer from a different regiment totaled up his whereabouts in 1916 and learned the following:

> I spent 65 days in the front line trenches, and 36 more in supporting positions

Leave and the Home Front

Soldiers believed that, in general, the average person back in Berlin, Paris, or London did not truly appreciate the struggles the men in the trenches were suffering on their behalf. Certainly there was a great deal of misinformation about the conditions at the front. Many of those at home honestly believed that the trenches were roomy underground shelters made of concrete, that fighting took place only during the day, or that war was nothing but heroism and glory. One British soldier twitted a friend for thinking that a periscope was some sort of musical instrument; he was amused, but many others resented the lack of awareness.

The problem could be exacerbated when men went home on leave. Most of the time, rest was accomplished only by rotating to the back of the lines, there to be held in reserve for a few days until the unit was deemed ready to return to the trenches. However, a man who had served for a long, uninterrupted stretch could usually count on a few days' leave. Most soldiers looked forward to these days as a vacation, a chance to escape the hardships of the trenches and an opportunity to see loved ones. Unfortunately, for some men the leave just served to underscore the differences between soldiers and those at home. In some ways, these men found themselves strangers in what should have been their own country; their thoughts were with the men back at the front. "It is very nice to be home again," mused a British soldier in John Ellis's *Eye-Deep in Hell*. "Yet am I at home? One sometimes doubts it."

close at hand. . . . In addition 120 days were spent in reserve positions near enough to the line to march up for the day when work or fighting demanded, and 73 days were spent out at rest. . . . 10 days were spent in Hospital . . . 17 days . . . on leave. . . . The 101 days under fire [that is, the days in the fire trench and in nearby support positions] contain twelve "tours" in the trenches varying in length from one to thirteen days. The battalion made sixteen in all during the year.[23]

Making the Transition

Moving one battalion into the fire trenches and another battalion out was usually complicated. For one thing, the transition almost always had to be accomplished at night; unless fighting was at a minimum and could be relied on to stay that way, it was too risky to bring large groups of men in or out of the trenches during daylight. And indeed there was danger any time whole fighting units moved back and forth close to enemy lines.

A more serious problem concerned the exchange of information between those leaving the trench and those newly arriving. Ideally, those on their way out would have spent plenty of time showing the newcomers the ropes. Even if the new battalion had been in the front lines before, the odds were good that they had not been in that particular stretch of the line. Many battalions also had new recruits or men who had recently returned from leave or medical treatment. Unless the battalion was returning from a short stay away, which was rarely the case—

Replacements often did not learn from the experiences of the trench veterans they replaced due to a need to conduct troop transfers quickly and at night.

the Allies and the Germans typically rotated troops through several different sectors of the front—the newcomers were in need of practical advice: where the supplies were kept, from what direction sniper fire could be expected, where the walls had a tendency to cave in, and so forth.

But if the transition was complete and all the men in a particular trench were rotated out, the newcomers rarely got what they needed. The battalion heading toward the rear was often in too much of a hurry to get away to be of much use. In some cases, the men in the front lines were already gone before the new arrivals reached their positions. In others, the newcomers received at best a few hints about staying as safe and dry as possible before the first battalion slipped through the communications trenches and away from the front.

Sometimes, of course, the change was not complete. Two or more units would be stationed in the fire trench at a time, but only one would be rotated out while the other stayed on. This system made the transition easier, since it assured that there would always be people who knew the ropes. The veteran soldiers often took the newcomers in hand, providing tips and moral support. "No bleedin' lights," a historian writes, summing up an experienced British soldier's words to a new arrival. "Let old Fritzie [slang for a German soldier] see a light . . . an[d] over comes an arf dozen shells knockin' yerall ter blazes."[24]

But even when some troops stayed on, the transition was rarely easy. Those who had been in the trenches for a while often resented the newcomers at first. Fair or not, the assumption was that the new arrivals had been living it up a good distance from the front while those already in the trenches had been suffering. When battalions stayed in the trenches for eight or ten days, it could take half the period before the new men were treated as equals by the old.

The Shape of the Day

The men's first responsibility of the morning was called stand-to, which usually took place a half-hour or so before dawn. Men stood on the step below the parapets, their rifles at the ready, while officers came through the trenches and checked to make sure they were as healthy as could be expected. The officers also took the opportunity to investigate the condition of the supplies, especially the amount of ammunition that remained, and to see what kind of repairs needed to be done to the trenches themselves. Stand-to was one part inspection and one part defense. Since dawn was often a time when attacks were staged, commanders on both sides liked having their men available and ready for action.

Following stand-to came breakfast. Breakfast was more than an opportunity to eat; it was also as close as most men got to having a genuine break from the rest of their duties. Except during times of intense battle, the two sides often worked out an unofficial cease-fire during breakfast. Shelling and shooting would vanish, or dwindle to a minimum, and men on both sides could relax. "Rifles would be cleaned," recalled one English soldier. "Three or four men would squat round and play nap [a card game]. . . . Some might start to sing quietly and others would join in."[25] Conditions were similar in German trenches.

Unfortunately, the end of breakfast also brought an end to relaxation and the informal truce. It was time to go back to work. Assuming that an attack was not scheduled and that the other side was not massing for an attack of its own, then the day continued as usual. Most often, the men in the rear trenches would fall to work sorting and moving supplies. In the meantime, the men in the fire trench would be divided into thirds, with the groups rotating among themselves every hour or two.

The first group was sent back to the parapets and assigned to sentry duty, or sentry-go as it was known to the British soldiers. Sentry duty was an unpleasant job under the best of circumstances. Most sentries were assigned the task of walking up and down the fire trench near the parapet, keeping a careful eye on the enemy across the neutral zone. Their main duty was to alert the other occupants of the trench in case of a massed attack, but sentries were also expected to keep tabs on enemy movement to the extent they were able.

Sentry duty was dangerous work. Unless a soldier used a periscope—and it was hard to use one while on the move—he had to be high enough to see over the top, which meant exposing himself to sniper fire. Moreover, sentries were expected to do what they could to defuse small enemy

Sentry duty exhausted soldiers, causing many to fall asleep. The penalty for sleeping on sentry duty could be as severe as death by firing squad.

bombs that made their way into the trench. Even when shooting was light, the sentry always had to be alert; a sudden burst of gunfire could leave him dead or seriously wounded.

Perhaps not surprising, sentry duty was also mentally and physically tiring. Being a sentry meant constantly scanning the horizon for a sign of something out of the ordinary. An hour or two of that was hard for most men to sustain. Many soldiers mentioned the sheer tedium of the responsibility in letters home, and more than a few sentries were discovered asleep on their feet at the back edge of their trenches. "For most of his time the average private was tired,"[26] wrote one English soldier, and sentry duty was a main reason why.

Falling asleep was particularly likely for sentries who did not move throughout the trench while carrying out their duties but instead stayed in one place and peered hopefully across the neutral zone from there. In some places, this type of sentry duty was more common. "Two men mount a post, two hours on, two hours sitting on the step," wrote one soldier, "ready with a blanket or overcoat to throw over bombs should they come over."[27] Whether the sentries were on the move or staying in one place, their duty was monotonous, dull, and taxing.

Not all men were needed as sentries. A second group helped ferry supplies back and forth between the fire trenches and the support trenches behind them. This work could be difficult or easy, depending on the weather, the general level of exhaustion, and the types and availability of supplies to be carried. Most of the time, though, this detail was physically and mentally wearying. Ammunition, food, and other materials were in constant demand in the front lines, and the narrow, winding communication trenches were not much fun to navigate.

"Resting"

While a third of the men served as sentries and another third went back and forth between the various trenches, the third group rested. Or so was the technical name for the activity. In fact, though, the men in this group got very little rest. These men were responsible for all kinds of jobs. "There was always something to be done," observed one soldier. "Digging, filling sandbags, carrying ammunition, scheming against water, strengthening the wire, resetting duckboards."[28] All these tasks fell into the laps of those who were—theoretically, at least— "resting."

Among the most important of these jobs involved the upkeep of the trenches. Since the trenches were open to the elements and enemy fire, they were constantly wearing away. Virtually every day something needed to be accomplished: a wall had to be reinforced, a set of sandbags replaced, a channel filling up with mud dug out to a proper depth. Whatever the chore, the men at rest were charged with the task of getting it done. Often it seemed that the work would never end. "The walls of the trenches caved in," wrote French soldier Marc Bloch despairingly. "It was constantly necessary to

Pay

Although many soldiers on both sides were volunteers, they were nevertheless paid for the work they did. Pay scales varied according to the army and to the type of work a man was trained to do. In the British army, for instance, regular soldiers received a base rate of a shilling a day, which could be supplemented if soldiers did extra tasks or worked with particular efficiency. Officers, on the other hand, might receive up to six times as much.

Other than using it for gambling, there was very little a soldier could do with money at the front itself. As a result, most soldiers were paid only when they rotated out of the trenches. Some soldiers saved as much of their money as they could, while others sent everything they could spare to their families at home. Others, though, were determined to spend their earnings as quickly as possible. Armed with French five-franc banknotes, British and French soldiers bought coffee, tobacco, good food, and occasionally the company of women as well.

In general, however, the wages were insufficient. Those men who were not officers could afford very little in the way of luxuries, and rarely could send much cash home to their families. The low pay added insult to injury in the minds of many soldiers during the war.

consolidate, to clear away, to board over and dig again."[29]

Maintaining the trenches may have been critical, but it was not the only job that had to be done. Carrying messages, helping the wounded, and distributing rations were also essential tasks, and those who were resting were usually called on first. Sometimes soldiers from this third group were sent forward to the listening posts at the front of the saps or told to take the place of a wounded sentry. Whatever jobs needed to be done generally fell to the men who were supposedly "resting."

The day continued with constant rotation between the three basic tasks: sentry duty, supplies detail, and the general heading of "resting." Soldiers grabbed sleep when they could, which was not often. Even when shelling and shooting were light, there was usually too much to do for the men to get much rest, although they tried.

The day came to a close the way it began: with a second stand-to, this one near dusk.

"Weariness Turns into Stupor"

Even after darkness, however, the workday did not end. To be sure, some of the more routine tasks ceased till morning. But the setting of the sun brought other chores into play. Under cover of the night, some soldiers would be pressed into service repairing barbed wire ripped apart by enemy shells or raiders. Sometimes, too, it made sense to enlarge a trench or to dig a new forward sap when the enemy could not see what was going on. While some soldiers slept, the activity around them continued.

And, of course, sentry-go continued. Usually, the watch was doubled, owing to the darkness and the ease of a stealth raid or other attack. At night, most soldiers agreed, the duty was much worse than during the day. Loneliness came into play in the black

night while other trenchmates slept, and in the darkness the imagination built every glimmer of light, every unexpected sound, into a probable attack. Exhaustion seemed to hit sentries much harder at night, as well. As one French soldier put it,

Soldiers learned to sleep when they could and where they could. Frontline conditions rarely provided the opportunity for lengthy rests.

> One hour, two hours, three hours, the time crawls as if paralysed. This guard duty will never end. Weariness turns into stupor. The man who was determined not to sleep can feel his eyes about to close, but he will not sleep. . . . There is always the rain, always the winter, always the shadows. The body van-

ishes, only the mind remains, watching and enduring; a little flame flickering in the shadows.[30]

Worse even than night sentry duty was night patrol. While sentry duty generally required soldiers to stay in or at least very near the trenches, patrol meant venturing out into no-man's-land. The goal was to crawl within earshot of the enemy's fire trenches, or as close as possible. With luck, they might capture someone or overhear valuable bits of conversation—more valuable, of course, for soldiers who spoke the other side's language. But perhaps the most important goal was to establish a presence in the neutral zone, signaling to the enemy that he could not simply march in whenever he felt like it.

A few soldiers relished the idea of patrol, or at least they said they did in letters home. But most did not. If sentry-go at night was alarming, then patrol was terrifying. As with sentry duty, perfectly normal sounds and sights became magnified into something sinister, but this was worse: In no-man's-land, there could be no illusion of safety. This was intensified by the flotsam that littered the zone: old unexploded grenades, pieces of barbed wire, cans, sheet metal, and more.

The worst of all, though, was the bodies of dead soldiers. These men had lost their lives on raids or in attacks, too far from the trenches for their comrades to bring the corpses in without risking their own lives. The bodies lay strewn across the neutral ground in various stages of decomposition, and soldiers on patrol never knew when they would crawl into the next one. All in all, patrol was one of the least favorite duties of the typical soldier, and it exacted a terrible psychological toll. "You . . . feel like an outlaw, exiled and untouchable," wrote a man from France. "You go out and come back—that is if you come back at all—a changed man."[31]

The duty soldiers dreaded most was patrol. While venturing into no-man's-land, these soldiers had to witness the carnage from the fighting.

Specialists

Not all men took part in the full round of duties. A few on each side were specialists, responsible for only one or two jobs—and expected to be very good at them. Snipers, for example, were usually exempt from most other chores. The most highly skilled of them could bring down any number of enemy soldiers in a short period of time, and so they were too valuable to use bearing supplies or standing lookout late at night. Similarly, a few units had engineers who took on the heaviest tasks of trench building. Given their frequent practice and careful training, these men could handle the task much more quickly and efficiently than the average soldier could; again, their skills were needed to construct trenches, so they were not asked to do much other than dig.

There were other specialists, too. Some units gave special work exemptions to men who showed expertise with weapons other than the rifle. Machine gunners, shell firers, and grenade throwers all stuck more or less to those duties in at least some British regiments. Germany offered relief from most routine chores to men who reached a certain rank in the army. A few Allied regiments formed small specialist organizations; one brigade, for instance, had its own wire unit, which took on the sole responsibility of stringing and repairing barbed wire in exchange for not taking on other daytime jobs. In many regiments, too, stretcher bearers—in charge of evacuating the wounded from the front lines to the safer medical clinics toward the rear—also performed that one job only.

Discipline

In an environment as dangerous and as tense as the trenches, a serious abdication of responsibility by one soldier could lead to the deaths of dozens. While most soldiers did manage to make the best of their miserable working conditions, not all could—or

---

"Like a Rabbit"

In this 1915 letter, quoted in *War Letters of Fallen Englishmen* an English soldier in France describes the trenches during wartime.

Here is the scene I shall remember always: A misty summer morning—I went along a sap-head running towards the German line at right-angles to our own. Looking out over the country, flat and uninteresting in peace, I beheld what at first would seem to be a land ploughed by the ploughs of giants. . . . Trenches rise up, grey clay, three or four feet above the ground. Save for one or two men—snipers—at the sap-head, the country was deserted. No sign of humanity—a dead land. And yet thousands of men were there, like rabbits concealed. The artillery was quiet; there was no sound but a cuckoo in a shell-torn poplar. Then, as a rabbit in the early morning comes out to crop grass, a German stepped over the enemy trench—the only living thing in sight. "I'll take him," says the man near me. And like a rabbit the German falls. And again complete silence and desolation.

would—do so. Those who did not carry out their duties could anticipate punishment, and military discipline was generally swift and severe.

Soldiers often ran afoul of military rules. As one historian of the British army put it, "Regulations were so numerous that all soldiers were likely to break some of them."[32] Most of these infractions, however, were relatively minor. A soldier might arrive late for a particular duty, light a match at the wrong time, or neglect to shine his shoes for an inspection. These men might be formally charged with a breach of conduct and summoned to appear before a commanding officer, or they might be admonished and released.

In most such cases, any punishment these offenders were given was fairly light: several days confined to the barracks, a few extra hours' hard labor, perhaps a short stretch in a military prison. A soldier could also have his pay suspended or his rank demoted. Some men were put on diets of bread and water; others were forced to drill almost constantly. As long as a man was not considered to be a danger to himself or his fellow soldiers, however, truly serious punishments were rare. Every man was needed in the trenches, and commanders thought twice about making one unavailable for duty for long. As a result, one common punitive measure was to suspend or reduce a man's next leave.

Some cases, however, were more serious. In the British army, about 3.5 percent of the men who served committed crimes significant enough to earn them a court-martial, in which they were imprisoned and brought before a military judge. The greatest number of these cases involved soldiers who were away from their companies without leave, although drunkenness was a close second. These men faced much more dire consequences if they were found guilty, including expulsion from the army and long-term imprisonment.

But these were not the worst offenses a soldier could commit. About one of every eight court-martialed troops had been arrested for insubordination—that is, because they had not followed the orders given to them. Drunkenness often had the same result as insubordination, but military authorities drew an important distinction between the two crimes. Although alcohol consumption might make a soldier unable to carry out duties, that inability could be put down to bad judgment rather than willful disobedience. But an outright refusal to follow orders was something else entirely. That refusal struck at the heart of the military system of unquestioning obedience from the soldiers.

Another, smaller percentage came before the court to answer charges of desertion. Sometimes the effects of this crime were indistinguishable from simply being absent without leave. But again, there was a difference. A soldier who tried to extend a leave for a few extra days could perhaps be forgiven, his offense chalked up to the stress of the war. Such an offense would be dealt with swiftly, but it did not seriously undermine the purpose of the army. In contrast, a soldier who simply climbed out of the trenches one night and left for good was flouting authority. As with insubordination, desertion was by far the greater crime.

Cowardice and Mutiny

Two other crimes were particularly significant during the war. One was cowardice. When the command was to hold position or press on, soldiers who ran were often charged with this offense. Some never returned. Others hung back during the heaviest fighting, hoping their actions would go unnoticed, and tried to rejoin their fellow troops later on. These men were often known as skulkers. "Skulkers were already numerous," wrote a German official about the last days of the war. "They reappeared as soon as the battle was over."[33]

A subcategory of cowardice encompassed soldiers who deliberately wounded themselves, hoping to make themselves useless for the remainder of the war and be sent home as a result. However, these cases amounted to only a small fraction of the court-martials. For the most part, soldiers on both sides fought bravely, even when the odds were stacked high against them. "I have seen men pale with fright," reported one British soldier. "But I never saw a man run the other way."[34]

The other serious offense—perhaps the most serious of them all—was mutiny. On several occasions, whole regiments refused to fight. The reason was usually a combination of fear, exhaustion, and hopelessness.

Typically, the rebels were men who had spent more than their share of days at the front, who had seen many of their comrades die in useless attacks on enemy trenches, and who no longer saw much point in continuing the war. "We will not harm you," said one French rebel, speaking for his regiment to their commanding officer. "But we will not obey you. The war must end."[35]

The punishments meted out for desertion, mutiny, and cowardice were stiff. In many cases, they cost soldiers their lives (although along the western front, the majority of men sentenced to die for these crimes eventually had their sentences commuted, or exchanged for a less harsh punishment). Death was by firing squad, a dozen soldiers selected to shoot at the condemned man. Most did not go quietly. "Help me, God! Where are you? Give me a chance—I've never had a chance!"[36] screamed one young man sentenced to die. The names of men who had been convicted of these high crimes and shot in this manner were often read aloud as a lesson and a warning to those who survived.

Sometimes, though, it was impossible to bring the culprits to justice. Deserters, for instance, often could not be caught. A few of these men defected to the other side, where they were safe enough for the time being. Others, especially French and Germans who knew the territory, slipped into the forests and made their way into safer areas without being seen again. The military simply did not have the resources to track all of them down. Similarly, cowardice in battle was very difficult to prove. Often, soldiers legitimately got lost, blacked out, or had other reasons for not having fought to the utmost, and many men's decision not to fight or charge went unnoticed.

The mutineers presented an especially interesting case. When one man refused to follow orders or go into battle, it was easy enough to make an example of him. His offense was clear: There were usually eyewitnesses, and no one else was willing to support him. When virtually an entire battalion refused to fight, however, the situation was quite different. Rounding up several hundred men was difficult, perhaps impossible, and proving the charge against any but the most vocal few was a complicated business. In the end, most authorities compromised, shooting or jailing only the ringleaders and often relaxing rules and conditions for the rest of the men.

What is remarkable about the First World War, however, is not the number of men who deserted, mutinied, or exhibited

Due to the terrible conditions on the front lines, many soldiers deserted or defected to the opposing side.

cowardice, but instead the number who did not. Despite terrible living conditions and unimaginable horrors, very few men ever committed more than a small infraction against the rules. The reasons for loyalty and compliance were many, ranging from courage to duty to patriotism. But perhaps the most common reason of all was a feeling of connectedness with other men in the pla-

toon. One officer wrote that his main motivations were "the honour of my battalion and its opinion of me."[37] His ideas were echoed in letters and diaries of thousands of soldiers on both sides. To help and protect their friends and be a member of the group in good standing: More than perhaps anything else, that desire helped keep men fighting.

Chapter 3

Injury, Illness, and Death

World War I saw astronomical numbers of deaths, numbers so large that most people at the time could not begin to comprehend them. More than a third of Serbians who fought died on the battlefield. Germany and Austria lost more than 3 million soldiers combined, most of them Germans. On the eastern front, Russia alone suffered approximately as many casualties. France lost over 1 million, Great Britain close to that figure. Many, though not all, of these losses were suffered in and near the trenches.

A large proportion of the soldiers who survived nevertheless suffered wounds. Some of these were minor, enough to get a soldier out of the front lines for a few days. Others were more substantial, injuries that required weeks or months of bed rest before a bone or internal organ was fully healed. And many wounds during the Great War were permanent and crippling. Soldiers went blind from poison gas or lost a leg to a grenade. By some estimates, half the men who saw action in the British front lines either were killed or suffered at least one wound during the conflict.

Disease, too, was rampant during the war. Hundreds of thousands of people were killed not by enemy guns but from illness, and hundreds of thousands more spent time in hospitals before recovering. As with wounds, some diseases were more serious than others. Pneumonia, tuberculosis, measles, and other illnesses spread rapidly through the tight quarters of the trenches. At best, they incapacitated the men for several days or weeks. At worst, they brought death.

Battle Deaths

To the men in the trenches, the possibility of death from battle was constant. The steady bombardment of the enemy artillery, the nightly patrols, the clouds of poison gas—all were a reminder that any soldier could die at virtually any moment. Men on both sides were well aware of their possible fate.

"Greetings from my grave in the earth,"[38] wrote one German soldier to a friend at home during a particularly heavy shelling. Not all soldiers were quite so forthright in their language, but many agreed with the sentiment.

Death was indeed everywhere. Nearly every man had a friend or companion who died, often while the man himself watched helplessly. "He was just blown to blazes," said one English infantryman to an officer, explaining what had become of a fellow soldier. "He was a chum of mine, sir, an' I seen 'im blown to blazes."[39] The images of men dying in such a way stayed with many of the survivors for the rest of their lives.

Most of the time death came quickly. A shell exploded or a rifle bullet pierced a heart or a brain, and the victim crumpled to the ground. As the saying goes, the man often never knew what had hit him. Bullets

Illnesses spread quickly in the close quarters of the trenches, and most soldiers suffered from injuries.

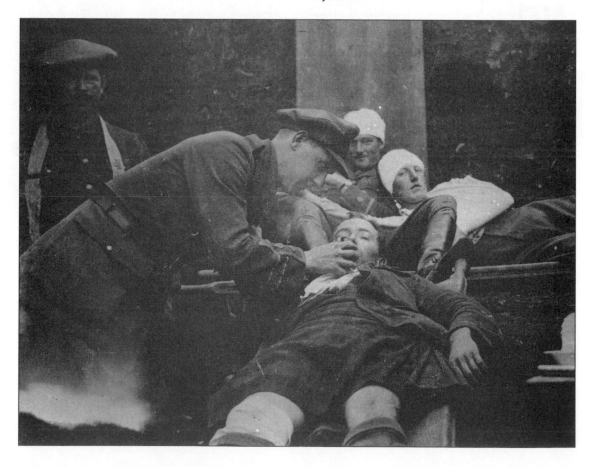

usually whizzed past quicker than the speed of sound, so if a man heard the bullet sing, the danger was over. In some cases, a shell or other heavy weapon exploded right on top of an unsuspecting soldier, shattering the body beyond hope of recognition. "Nothing but a mass of mud and blood,"[40] mourned one French soldier about a comrade killed by an artillery shell.

But the quick deaths, horrible as they might be, were the easier ones. Other times the deaths were long and drawn out. When possible, those still alive came to the aid and comfort of the dying, even telling lies to ease the pain of the man's final moments. "One knew them all so well and under a bright sun it looked too horrible," wrote an English officer about a shelling that left many of his outfit's soldiers mortally wounded.

[One] poor lad with his two feet off was . . . obviously dying. . . . I wiped his mouth and he said quietly and clearly "Shall I live, sir?" "Live?" I said. "Good lord yes. You'll be right as rain when you're properly dressed [bandaged] and looked after." "Thank you, sir," he said. . . . He died as they were getting him onto the ambulance.[41]

Soldiers hoped for a quick death, dreading a wound that would cause them to linger in agony.

The sheer random nature of the deaths that were suffered made the fact of death especially hard for men in the trenches to take. It was often a matter of inches and luck. One soldier left his post at the end of

Expected to Kill

For most soldiers, the greatest psychological stress of trench life was the fear of being killed. The danger of death or serious injury from sniper fire, from artillery shells, and from hand grenades was constant and unpredictable, and the continuous worry wore many men down. However, for some men, an even greater source of stress was the fact that they were expected to kill. These soldiers were troubled by the idea of going out and shooting a stranger with whom they had no personal quarrel. In some cases, the problem was the notion of killing at all. "I can imagine nothing more horrible than suddenly to feel the primitive passion for slaughter let loose in one," wrote a British soldier who had yet to take part in a battle, as quoted in *War Letters of Fallen Englishmen*,

"and to know that one was more than at liberty to give it full rein."

A few soldiers went to great mental lengths to avoid having to deal with their need to be violent. This poem, written by a soldier and quoted in Ellis, *Eye-Deep in Hell*, is a good example:

They ask me where I've been,
And what I've done and seen
But what can I reply,
Who knows it wasn't I,
But someone just like me,
Who went across the sea,
And with my head and hands
Killed men in foreign lands . . .
Though I must bear the blame
Because he bore my name.

a shift, and the moment he walked away, a shell hit the spot where he had been standing. Two men sat next to each other, and a sudden hail of bullets killed one and left the other untouched. One man died of a bullet ricocheting off the back wall of the trench, while another escaped certain death when a shell turned out to be a dud. Some men took their survival as a sign of God's grace, but others were less sure. "He [God] knows I didn't deserve it a fraction as much as the poor splendid heroes who are killed,"[42] mused one lucky British soldier.

It was also true that many men, especially in the early days of the war, did not completely understand the grim reality of war. For some, joining the army seemed like the most exciting activity imaginable. To dress up in a uniform and carry a gun seemed like a gigantic game of cops and robbers or hide-and-seek, only with more competitors and bigger playing fields, to say nothing of getting to fight for one's own country. "I *adore* War," wrote English soldier Julian Grenfell in a letter to his mother during October 1914. "It is like a big picnic without the objectlessness of a picnic. . . . Nobody grumbles at one for being dirty."[43]

Grenfell's attitude was far from unusual. Many other soldiers felt the same way. But for most who served in the trenches, reality soon sank in: This was not a game, and the consequences of losing were real. In another letter a few weeks later, Grenfell mentioned his increasing understanding that war could indeed be horrible. Another English soldier had begun the war with feelings similar to Grenfell's. Before long, however, he had changed his outlook considerably. "I shall never look at warfare as fine or sporting again," he wrote. "It reduces men to shivering beasts."[44]

Dealing with the Dead

Methods for disposing of corpses from battle varied considerably throughout the war. When possible, bodies were buried right away, usually in shallow graves at some distance behind the trenches. That was easy enough during slack periods in the fighting, when a man killed by a sniper bullet might be the only casualty of the day. But it was much more difficult during times of heavy shelling, or when the bodies were of men killed in the neutral zone. In those cases, it was often too difficult or dangerous to spare men to retrieve the body and bring it to a final resting place.

As a result, it was common for corpses to remain where they had fallen for days, weeks, or even months. Gradually they sank into the mud and grit of no-man's-land, or sometimes in the trenches themselves. Usually they did not remain completely undisturbed, however. Instead, soldiers gradually carried away the dead man's boots, jacket, or anything else that could be reused. Some referred to this practice as looting and disapproved of it. Others, more tolerant and more aware of the hardships faced by the survivors, simply called it scavenging.

For health purposes as well as for humanitarian reasons, soldiers did try to remove their dead from the fields when they could. Once in a while, a cease-fire would be called for expressly that purpose. But more

A timely burial was unlikely for soldiers killed in the field. The dangers of land mines, snipers, and unexploded shells held back the burial details.

often, men would try to find a lull in the action and remove the corpses they could reach. The work, everyone agreed, was appalling. Badly decomposed bodies turned men's stomachs, and the stench was overwhelming. An Englishman who had the misfortune to take part in one of these burial details noted that the men had to stop at frequent intervals to vomit.

Even worse was trying to properly identify the men's bodies. Most soldiers carried dog tags identifying their names and battle units, but dog tags sometimes became separated from their owners, especially if the body had been lying in the same place for a long time. Moreover, shells sometimes obliterated the dog tag as well as the owner. Many men were officially listed as "missing" because it was not possible to determine for sure whether they were among the dead.

Relatives of dead and missing soldiers usually received official correspondence from their country's government. In some cases, they also got a comforting letter from the man's commander or from a close friend of the man who died. Such letters usually mentioned how well liked the man had been among his comrades, and explained how much he had grown as a person and as a soldier during his time at the front. Occasionally, too, they described the man's death, which in the letters frequently came gloriously, honorably, and most of all with merciful quickness. No doubt some of the men actually did die in this manner, but in most cases the description was pure fiction, designed to console the family.

Wounds

Like death, a wound could come at any moment for a soldier in the trenches. A shell might explode too far away to kill a man but close enough to blow shrapnel into his side or head. A sniper bullet might graze an arm or lodge in a leg. Gas attacks often failed to kill, but caused seared lungs and scarred flesh. Of course, some men died from their wounds. That was especially true of those who were hit in the abdomen, the head, or the chest. Most of the wounded soldiers, however, survived.

Being hit was not necessarily unpleasant. Oddly, the more serious the wound, the less pain the victim often felt. Relatively minor wounds to the hands and feet could hurt intensely, but more serious wounds often did not announce their presence through the nervous system. "Blast it, I've been hit," wrote one British soldier, describing the sensation of a head wound. "I wonder by what? Couldn't have been a shell as there wasn't an explosion. Damnation. Look at the blood pouring on my new tunic."[45] It was not until later that he realized what had happened.

Still, any wound might possibly spell disaster. That was especially true during an attack or at any other time when a man was hit in the neutral zone. During a charge, attackers were forbidden to stop to help an injured fellow soldier. Moreover, in the heat of the moment, soldiers often did not realize that someone needed help. A man who was badly wounded during a charge had little recourse but to lie where he had fallen and wait for his division's stretcher bearers.

It could be a very long wait. The stretcher bearers were known for their courage and selflessness, but they were unarmed and could not usually venture onto the field without a cease-fire or a covering attack. Even men who were quite close to the trenches were sometimes completely unreachable. A wounded man's best bet was to cry for help at regular intervals; if he did not keep calling, he ran the risk of being overlooked when the medical crews did arrive.

Soldiers were trained to leave the wounded where they lay until the fighting ended. This practice led to an even greater death toll.

Even if the man's cries were heard quickly and it was possible to send out a crew of stretcher bearers, his suffering was not over. The British army provided only four stretcher bearers for each company. These were supplemented when possible by regular troops, but still it often took three or four men to transport a single wounded soldier. At Passchendaele in Belgium, one observer wrote, it could take ten men to drag a stretcher any distance at all. Mud, shell craters, and the twists and turns of the trenches all conspired to make the two-man stretcher a myth. "The trenches were knee-deep in glueing mud," wrote one stretcher carrier, "and it was the hardest work I have ever done."[46]

In the meantime, the wounded men sought protection as best they could. Some dragged themselves into shell craters, hoping to be less visible targets for the enemy. Others lacked the strength to do even this. Once they were shot, however, time was an even greater enemy than the German or Allied soldiers in the opposite trenches. After battles, the cries of the wounded gradually got softer and weaker as more and more gave up the fight. Still, some men survived for astonishingly long periods of time. One man was hit in the chest and was rescued—alive—four days later. He had survived partly by using his cap to capture rainwater for drinking.

Treatment

The first stop for a wounded man was an improvised medical shelter set up in a back trench. There, soldiers received very basic emergency care. The medics who worked in the shelter administered anesthetic to badly injured men; they also dressed wounds and performed amputations if leaving the injured limb attached seemed likely to cause death. Some men needed to go no further,

but most of the wounded were quickly sent on to the next stop, the so-called casualty clearinghouse.

Located a few miles behind the last trench, the casualty clearinghouse was a hut or tent that served as a sort of field hospital. The main function of the clearinghouse was to determine the seriousness of a man's injuries. The men who came in were divided into three groups. The most severely hurt stayed where they were; they were too sick to be moved any further. The least dangerously wounded also stayed, receiving the medical treatment necessary to get them back to the front as soon as possible. The rest were shipped back to regular hospitals far from the fighting. More than 2 million English troops were sent back to England for further medical care.

Conditions in the clearinghouses were not good. The field hospitals were noted for dim light, a perpetual shortage of staff, and no shortage at all of patients. One military surgeon described the scene:

Into the tent are borne on stretchers or come wearily stumbling, figures in khaki wrapped in blankets or coats, bandaged or splinted. All of them are caked in mud or stiff with blood and dust and sweat. Labels of their injuries are attached. Many are white and cold and lie still. . . . I have never seen such dreadful wounds.[47]

The wounds were indeed dreadful. The increased firepower of World War I's weapons damaged flesh and bone in ways unknown during earlier wars.

By modern standards, the care given at these clearinghouses was appallingly poor. The problem was not with the doctors and their level of skill but with the medical knowledge of the time. There were no X rays, so bullets and other fragments tended to stay in the body, often resulting in infection. Antibiotics were unknown. Amputation was the standard—indeed, the only—treatment for serious wounds to the leg or arm.

Though some anesthetics were in use, most were so poorly understood that many patients were given overdoses, with disastrous results such as coma or death. Still, the doctors did what they could with the knowledge they had. Surgeons in these hospitals pioneered several new procedures—use of

Wounded soldiers were first taken to a medical shelter in a rear trench, and then on to a clearing center where they were divided into groups ranked by the seriousness of their injuries.

anesthesia, taking X rays, blood transfusions, early forms of plastic surgery—which saved lives both during the war and afterward. Many soldiers survived their wounds only because of the skill and expertise of the military doctors.

It should be noted that many soldiers welcomed small injuries that would incapacitate them without doing serious permanent damage. English soldiers called these "blighty" wounds. Blighty was an affectionate name for England, and such a wound often resulted in the soldier being sent home. "A broken arm is better than a hole in the guts," says a character in *All Quiet on the Western Front*, a novel by German writer and World War I veteran Erich Maria Remarque, "and many a man would be thankful enough for such a chance of finding his way home again."[48]

Disease

The trenches of World War I were breeding grounds for disease. Men were tightly packed together, so any contagious illness caught by one soldier was likely to infect many more. Poor medical treatment also led to the spread of disease. So did exhaustion, which affected numerous soldiers at the front much of the time. But the greatest single cause of sickness was the condition of the trenches.

In a word, the trenches were filthy. One problem was rat infestation. "Huge rats," wrote one Canadian recruit in wonderment that the animals could grow so large. "So big they would eat a wounded man if he couldn't defend himself." Rats roamed freely through the zigzagged lines, biting men and carrying insect-borne disease. Entirely at home in the trenches and afraid of nothing,

Hospital Life

Workers in military hospitals could be callous—not because the doctors and nurses were indifferent but because there were so many wounded that medical staffers could not grow overly involved in any one case. The situation was nicely summed up by Erich Maria Remarque in his novel *All Quiet on the Western Front.* The narrator is a teenage soldier in the German army. He is begging a doctor to help his dying friend Franz Kemmerich, who has just undergone an amputation.

[The doctor] sniffs: "How should I know anything about it, I've amputated five legs today"; he shoves me away, says to the hospital-orderly "You see to it," and hurries off to the operating room.

I tremble with rage as I go along with the orderly. The man looks at me and says: "One operation after another since five o'clock this morning. You know, today alone there have been sixteen deaths—yours is the seventeenth. There will probably be twenty altogether—"

I become faint, all at once I cannot do any more. I won't revile him any more, it is senseless, I could drop down and never rise up again.

We are by Kemmerich's bed. He is dead. . . . The orderly pokes me in the ribs, "Are you taking his things with you?" I nod.

He goes on: "We must take him away at once, we want the bed. Outside they are lying on the floor."

they clambered across sleeping soldiers and sought out food in men's pockets. Rats contributed greatly to the problem of rampant disease at the front.

Though not as big as the rats, lice caused illness too. Virtually no one escaped the ravages of these tiny insects. "There was no getting rid of them," wrote one soldier. "They would breed on you, and no matter how often you changed yourself, you would be just as bad the next day."[50] Body lice were not just a nuisance. Some caused skin problems or carried typhoid fever. Others infected men with a disease called trench fever. Trench fever was poorly understood at the time—markers included chills, fevers, and intense joint and muscle pain—and British army officials suspected that some of the sufferers were faking their symptoms to get out of the trenches. But the disorder was real enough.

The weather was perhaps an even greater health issue. Soldiers froze in the winter and baked in the summer heat. In cold weather, men came down with a condition called "trench foot," which turned out to be a form of frostbite caused by lack of exercise, poorly fitting boots, and extreme cold. Treatment often required the removal of several toes. Being cold and wet

Poor drainage and sanitation in the trenches led to a variety of illnesses and injuries.

also led to nephritis, a kidney disease. Most soldiers did not die from these illnesses, but they did lead miserably painful existences.

The worst problem of all, though, was the mud and slime at the bottom of the trenches. The frantic pace of life in the trenches meant that proper hygiene was usually out of the question. "I have not washed for a week," wrote one soldier, "or had my boots off for a fortnight."[51] The disposal of human waste away from the lines was also difficult. Soldiers constructed latrines within the walls of the trenches, but these often overflowed when fighting became furious, which was frequent. As a result, dysentery, cholera, and other stomach disorders were rampant.

The sickest soldiers spent time in hospitals. Most others were kept in the front lines as long as they could stay awake and were not in imminent danger of death. Commanders usually suffered a shortage of manpower, so they were reluctant to part with any man, even one operating at less than full efficiency. Among those sent to hospitals, only a very few died—perhaps 1 percent of English soldiers, according to one study. Still, the appalling conditions of the trenches caused needless suffering for men on both sides.

Coping

Soldiers developed ways of dealing with the horrors of the trenches and the knowledge that they could be the next to die. Some grew reflective and pondered the meaning and purpose of life and death. A few of these men decided that the sacrifice was justified by the cause of patriotism or some other great individual glory. Others, however, were more introspective. "We had to collect what had been a man the other day and put it in a sandbag and bury it," wrote a schoolteacher-turned-soldier in a letter to a friend. "And less than two minutes before he had been laughing and talking and *thinking*. . . ."[52] The sentence trailed off, and the letter ended there.

Some of these men were also struck by the apparent wastefulness of so many of the deaths. During most of the conflict, battle lines barely moved at all. The fact that no progress ever seemed to be made often led men to question the purpose of what they were doing—and the risks they took. Dying a glorious death might have been one thing if the death helped bring the enemy to its knees. But as the death toll mounted, it was harder and harder to believe that the deaths were for any greater purpose.

More significantly, death caused some men to think of the enemy in very human terms. Both sides had effective propaganda machines that stirred up public sentiment against the enemy, often quite literally demonizing him. "Our valiant ones are fighting the Devil,"[53] exclaimed one British writer. For the most part, soldiers accepted this image. But as the conflict dragged on, many began to question its truth. The dead enemy soldiers they saw in the trenches and in the neutral zone were men very much like themselves. "All the world over," mused a British soldier, "a boy is a boy and a mother is a mother."[54]

Others bitterly mourned their fallen friends, allowing themselves to feel grief and sorrow. "Hans is dead," wrote one German soldier. "Fritz is dead. Wilhelm is dead.

There are many others."[55] Some men put up small markers to indicate where fellow soldiers had died. These were usually wooden crosses with inscriptions along the lines of "In loving memory of . . ." or "Rest in peace, beloved brother." Occasionally the sentiment turned mawkish, but the fact was that death *was* sad; it was healthy to mourn.

Still, many soldiers found that they could not think too much about their fallen comrades. The circumstances of the war—the duties, the attacks, the incessant pounding of the shells—demanded too much of their time and attention. "Life is a curious thing in war," mused one soldier, regretting that he did not think more often of the men who had died.

Men who you like and with whom you have been close suddenly get struck down. You feel sorry for them and for a fleeting instant you feel their poignant loss. But presently vain regrets are cast aside and one plunges back into the activities of the present; new people take their place and life goes on. It is no matter of callousness.[56]

In many cases, too, the easiest response to the constancy of death was to laugh about it. Macabre humor abounded in the trenches. "What's the point of scratching your head?" asked a French soldier in 1916. "A shell will do it very well."[57] Army slang terms often reflected this strategy of dealing

"Sure, It's Fun!"

The poetry of World War I took many different forms. Some of the verses were unabashedly patriotic, seeing the war as a battle between the forces of good and evil. "Leap, waves of England! Boastful be, / And fling defiance in the blast!" commanded one such poem quoted in J. W. Cunliffe's *Poems of the Great War*. Others were more reflective, thinking about the human side of the conflict, as in this excerpt from a poem written in the fall of 1914: "Tumult and roaring of the incessant gun; / Dead men and dying, trenches lost and won."

A much smaller group of poems took on a satiric tone. One example, by American poet Richard Butler Glaenzer, is called "Sure, It's Fun!" Glaenzer began his poem with a quotation from a boys' magazine of the time, which read, "What fun to be a soldier!" These are Glaenzer's last two verses, also quoted in *Poems of the Great War*.

"Oh, it's fun to be a soldier! Oh, it's fun, fun, fun,

To catch the silly enemy and get 'em on the run;
To here and there blow off a head with just a bit of chuckling lead;
To bayonet a foolish bloke at hide-and-seek in trench and smoke;
To shoot, shoot, shoot, till they've got no legs to scoot!
Fun?——Sure, it's fun, just the finest ever, son!

God, it's fun to be a soldier! Oh, it's fun, fun, fun,
To lie out still and easy when your day's sport's done;
With not a thing to worry for, nor anything to hurry for;
Not hungry, thirsty, tired, but a hero much admired,
Just dead, dead, dead, like Jack and Bill and Fred!
Fun?–Sure, it's fun, just the finest ever, son!"

with the reality of the war. English soldiers, for example, breezily referred to the deadly German machine guns as "Fritz's typewriters." Similarly, men cheerfully sang about the days ahead, when they would be dead and worms would eat their corpses on the battlefields. To joke about the war and its destruction could make it seem less powerful.

But much of the time, the jokes ended when men died. To talk in general terms about Fritz's typewriters and to sing about worms eating dead bodies was good fun, most soldiers agreed; still, things were different when death suddenly became a reality. "Last night, turning a traverse [passage in the trenches] sharply, I almost stepped on a Horrible Thing [that is, a corpse]," wrote a British soldier. "We can afford to laugh at corpses, if we did not know them when alive. . . . But when a German bullet strikes a man in the head and takes away his scalp and a lot of his brains clean away, and still lets him live for two hours, the joke is no more."[58]

Shell Shock

In many cases, the stress of life in the trenches could not be managed by any of these strategies. During times of intense barrages, many men came close to breaking down. "Oh, Christ, make it stop," a soldier from England remembered thinking during an exceptionally heavy shelling. "It must stop because I can't bear it any more."[59] Another young soldier, full of bravado, had a dud German shell land in the muck near him; according to an eyewitness, the recruit could not stop shaking for the next twenty-four hours.

Soldiers generally found ways of reducing the stress. But in some cases that was simply impossible. The never-ending dodging of shells and listening to constant gunfire took its toll. For some men, it brought on a psychological condition known to French soldiers as *le cafard*, or a kind of listless depression. As one soldier described it, "It is a lowering of morale that takes hold of you. Everything looks black. You are tired of life itself."[60]

Le cafard was bad enough, but sometimes the effect of the stress could be much worse. Men who were asked to make countless charges often came quite close to insanity. "Haggard, bloodshot-eyes," one eyewitness wrote about a line of soldiers returning from an exceptionally grim series of attacks; "slouching on beyond fatigue and hope . . . desperate-faced . . . slobbering and blowing."[61] There was nothing especially unusual about soldiers who looked and acted this way; during times of heavy stress, most men reacted as these men did.

In some soldiers, though, stress brought about a breakdown commonly known as shell shock or battle fatigue. Shell shock, in its extreme forms, was easy enough to recognize. Men clawed at their faces and screamed frantically; men rocked wordlessly back and forth; men smiled at the wrong moments, said the wrong things, shouted orders to invisible friends. Some cases were less obvious, but the results were the same: The men, overwhelmed by the dangers, the conditions, and the responsibilities of the trench war, had lost touch with reality. Mentally and

emotionally, they could no longer carry out all their functions as part of the army.

Shell shock was slow to take hold of the troops. As it began to grow among the soldiers, army leaders dismissed its importance; they accused the men who contracted it of cowardice, of fakery, or of moral and physical weakness. Even if it were real, officials argued, it was a physical ailment, created when an exploding shell affected the mechanism of the brain (hence the name "shell shock"). That it might have to do with the stress of battle did not occur to these men. After all, officials pointed out, nothing like shell shock had been seen in previous wars.

But of course no previous war had been fought under the circumstances that prevailed in World War I, where battles raged for days and there was no rest. And as time went on, an ever-growing number of soldiers came down with the disorder. Many of

Shell shock, a mental breakdown caused by the intensity and duration of battle, had not been observed prior to World War I. Pictured are shell shock victims recovering at a Red Cross hospital.

these men had been war heroes, athletes, upper-class recruits full of swash and buckle. As a result, it grew harder for officials to blame the shell-shocked soldiers for their own condition.

To be sure, unless the symptoms were unmistakable, both sides were reluctant to diagnose their soldiers as shell-shocked. Perhaps one out of fifty English soldiers was eventually classified with the disorder, but many historians believe the actual incidence was significantly higher. Some of these men got better on their own, especially after a period of rest far from the front lines. Rotating out of the trenches probably saved many of these men from permanent insanity. Even among those who were hospitalized, though, most recovered enough to return to the front lines.

Still, the war exacted a terrible psychological toll on its soldiers. For too many, shell shock destroyed their lives. Some shell-shocked men were shot for cowardice or insubordination, their commanders unable or unwilling to recognize the mental origins of their actions. Thousands more, unhurt physically, were sent home and never again resumed normal life. Many of these survived for decades after the conflict was over. Sixty years following the war's end, one British historian wrote,

Each week I see in Leavesden mental hospital, the largest in England, a man whose memory is perfect, within the limits of his great age, to 1917. Thereafter he can remember nothing. An explosion had wiped the recording mechanism from his life and hospitalized him from that day to this. [62]

This man was proof that the casualties of the war went well beyond amputations, beyond trench fever, even beyond death. For many men, the fearsome circumstances of trench warfare made basic sanity a question mark.

Supplies and Survival

The trenches did not exist in a vacuum. The men who manned the guns and the sentry posts required food, clothing, ammunition, and more. Thousands of pounds of materials were consumed at the front lines every single day of the war. To prepare for the 1916 Battle of Verdun, for example, the French used thirty-five hundred trucks to carry four thousand tons of supplies to the front, along with several thousand men newly enlisted or being rotated back to the trenches.

Getting the supplies and the soldiers there was quite a task. Under the best of circumstances, it was possible to map out effective supply routes and systems that would quickly and efficiently get the troops what they needed. But most of the time, conditions were not ideal. In such cases, the war effort suffered—and more often than not, the men did too.

Indeed, waging war required thousands of people who did not necessarily have a role in the fighting. Besides the doctors and the stretcher carriers, there were also drivers, cooks, sewing machine operators, and many other workers, each of whom was vital to the war effort. One British writer of the time estimated that thirteen support staffers were necessary to support one man fighting in the front lines. While the exact numbers may have been slightly off, the sentiment was not.

The trench system rarely worked to the soldiers' advantage, but it did where supplies were concerned. On the western front, the trenches served as an almost permanent dividing line between the two sides. Everything to the east of the line was held by the Central Powers, and everything west of it by the Allies. In earlier wars of movement, armies often outdistanced their supply sources. Many times soldiers were trapped far into enemy territory with no means of survival except foraging, or living off the land. By contrast, the armies of the western front during World War I generally had little difficulty maintaining contact with their supply bases.

Delivering supplies to the front line proved a difficult task for the support units stationed in the rear.

Still, the difficulties associated with getting the supplies to the men were notoriously arduous. All the territory to the west of the line was French, but that was little use to the French soldiers in places where only one small dirt road led from the interior of the country to the trench system. Poor transportation led to bottlenecks and traffic jams. As one eyewitness wrote about a heavily used French road, "The mighty [war] machine must go on and on without any stoppage. If an axle breaks or a wheel crocks up, the loaded wagon, bus, tank, whatever it may be, is shoved into the nearest ditch and traffic is resumed."[63]

Moreover, battle often made it difficult or impossible to move supplies. It was too dangerous to transport items through the communication trenches when the shells were falling thick and fast. Depending on the range of the enemy artillery, it was sometimes hazardous just to bring the supplies to the rearmost trench. Not only did the movers stand a large chance of dying, but the supplies themselves could easily be destroyed. And personnel could not be spared when an attack seemed imminent. When heavy shelling lasted a few hours, it was usually not a problem to postpone delivery of the supplies in question, but when battles went on for several days, as many did, the lack of fresh supplies began to take its toll.

Kits and Other Supplies

Each soldier on the western front was issued a backpack, or "kit," containing the basic necessities of soldier life. Many of the contents would be supplemented by regular deliveries of new supplies, but others would not. Exactly what was in these kits varied considerably according to the soldier's country of origin. A kit generally contained a rifle and plenty of rounds of ammunition. Later in the war, it also typically included a gas mask. These were the basic tools of the soldier's trade, and no soldier ventured into the trenches without them.

But weapons and protection from gas were not all the soldiers carried. The standard French soldier's kit weighed about sixty pounds, not counting the rifle, the bullets, and the mask. One observer declared that the French carried "their trunk and even their cupboard"[64] on their backs. Among many other items, French soldiers were given candles, soap, and a digging tool to help them burrow more deeply into the trenches. They also had a small lamp, a blanket, a tarpaulin, and a pair of slipperlike shoes. Finally, the kit included several emergency foodstuffs, including canned beef, biscuits, dried soup, and a bag of sugar. Though these foods were not usually very palatable, especially after several days in trench conditions, they would do in a pinch.

Soldiers from all countries also carried around a variety of personal possessions. Some of these were obtained legitimately: They had been brought from home at the beginning of the conflict or sent by friends and relatives. Others were "souvenirs" collected from enemy prisoners, and occasionally from corpses. "I have already been souvenired,"[65] remarked a German prisoner-of-war, who was asked if he had any valuables on his person. A few "souvenirs" had been stolen from fellow soldiers or pilfered from the general supplies—both of which happened more often than army officials liked to admit.

The soldiers' possessions were varied. The literate men carried writing paper and pencils and letters they had received. Many brought photographs of their loved ones. Others preferred to squirrel away medicines, small tools such as knives and scissors, or extra clothing, and still others carried decks of cards or dice for games. These items were carried wherever a soldier could find room. In a few cases they interfered with the carrying out of duties, as with the French soldier who loaded eighteen pockets with materials of all sorts. Most of the time, though, the soldier willingly put up with a little extra weight in his backpack in exchange for the comfort and ease the items provided him.

Food

Of all the supplies provided to the men in the trenches, food was the most important and the most exasperating. By the end of 1915, the food was cooked in massive rolling kitchens stationed as close to the front as the armies dared to put them. These kitchens were enormous. "There is a bakery," reported a visitor to the front, "where a Master Baker, in charge of a thousand men, bakes 350,000 2-lb. loaves every day."[66] Ideally, the kitchens would turn out enough food to support the men in that sector, and the food would be rapidly transported to the front lines.

Each army allotted its soldiers a specific daily ration of food. Although the exact items in the menu might vary from day to day, the nutritional value was supposed to remain the same. For example, each front-line soldier in the major armies of the western front—German, English, French, and

Although each soldier was supposed to receive a specific daily ration of food, soldiers rarely received what they were promised.

"To Hell with Beans and Stew!"

Noted American songwriter Irving Berlin wrote several successful songs about army life. Among them was a ditty titled "Oh, How I Hate to Get Up in the Morning," which poked light-hearted fun at the tribulations of being a soldier. American soldiers during the war certainly enjoyed Berlin's song, but they preferred to sing their own words to the tune he had created. One such parody was directed at army food in particular; it was called "Oh, How I Hate to Go into the Mess Hall."

"Oh, how I hate to go into the mess hall!
Oh, how I long for the foods at home!
For it isn't hard to guess
Why they call the meals a mess—
You've got to eat beans, you've got to eat beans,
You've got to eat beans in the army.
Some day I'll murder the cook in the kitchen;
Some day I'll throw him into the lake.
And when the bloomin' war is through
I'll say: 'To hell with beans and stew!'
And spend the rest of my pay on steak."

American composer Irving Berlin wrote several songs that poked fun at the harsh conditions World War I soldiers were forced to endure.

(later during the conflict) American—was supposed to have between four and five thousand calories daily. Similarly, each soldier in the American army could expect a pound and a quarter of meat every day, while German troops made do with half a pound less. On the other hand, the German army provided its troops with a greater vegetable ration than did any of the other countries.

Those amounts, however, were valid mainly in theory. In practice, soldiers rarely received exactly what the guidelines called for. Mostly, they got less, and occasionally they got much less. There were several reasons for the shortages. One was a general problem of food shortages across Europe. Some of these were due to the loss of prime agricultural land in areas of fighting; others were the result of poor harvests in areas undisturbed by the war. Still others stemmed from widespread disruption of trade. Germany suffered more from this problem than the Allies did, but every nation had food shortages to some degree.

The more significant problems, though, involved the supply system. The food had to be carried to the rolling kitchens on wagons or trucks, and many of these vehicles never arrived. They became stuck in heavy traffic or bogged down on muddy roads; they broke down and could not quickly be repaired; they moved so slowly that the food they carried spoiled and had to be thrown out. Even foods that did reach the kitchens met similar fates once cooked and on their way to the front.

Sometimes, too, the food simply disappeared. Crooked officers commandeered it and sold it at inflated prices for their own personal gain; hungry civilians pilfered much of the cargo before it could arrive in

On Leadership

English soldiers ate plenty of a food called Maconachie, a canned mixture of meat and vegetables. This tongue-in-cheek advertisement for the product, quoted in Ellis, *Eye-Deep in Hell,* demonstrated the typical soldier's feelings about the food. Note especially the names of the men quoted.

"Read what our Soldier Boys say.

'Please forward me the residential address of Mr. Maconachie, as when next on leave I wish to call and pay my compliments.'

—WILL BASHEM (Corpl.)

'Words are inadequate to express my delight when I observe your famous rations upon the mess table.'

——S. A. R. CASTIC (Bombdr.) [bombardier] . . .

'Nothing more readily appeases the capacious appetites of my platoon than your ever-ready dinners.'

——D. A. M. (Cook)"

the trenches. Alternatively, the food could go to waste. The cooks were not necessarily of equal skill. Often, whole boxes of food would have to be thrown out because it was burned beyond recognition by an inexperienced chef.

For the men in the trenches, the result of this loss was frequently a gnawing hunger. French propaganda officials once cheerfully announced that every soldier at the front lines got at least two good meals a day. The goal was to make the people at home believe that matters were organized and the troops were being properly cared for. The general public may have accepted the information, but the soldiers themselves knew better. The officials received an estimated 200,000 letters from irate troops demanding to know where their two good meals were.

In some cases, where supply problems were compounded by heavy shelling that never seemed to let up, men approached starvation diets. "Three biscuits a day," wrote a soldier who served in the trenches at Gallipoli in the Middle East. "No bacon or sometimes a little and a very little stew. For dinner we got a little cheese but only a bite."[67] During another ferocious battle, this one on the western front, support staffers had to crawl as close as they could to a besieged trench and throw rations inside. The men had already choked down the rations that had been issued as part of their kits, and they had no immediate means of escape from the trench.

But quantity was not the real problem with the food. Except in rare cases, men

Although American soldiers often suffered from hunger, they still received more food than many civilians. At times, soldiers enjoyed food prepared by Salvation Army workers.

did not starve in the trenches. Nor do there appear to have been many more instances of malnutrition than there would have been in the general population. Many European peasants of the time barely had enough to eat themselves; in good times and bad, the poorest in each nation often went hungry. World War I, of course, was far from a time of plenty, so the condition of the peasants was reduced accordingly. Even in the German army, where the twelve-ounce daily meat ration was soon reduced to ten and then six, the men in the front lines still ate better than most civilians did.

"A Change Would Not Displease Them"

The greater problem with food was quality. Letters and diaries of soldiers in all armies contain frequent disparaging references to the food. In some cases, the problem was the sameness of the menu. "The basic meal," mourned a French writer, "consists, morning and evening [of rice]. Our friends beg us to declare that a change would not displease them."[68] English troops received a special ration of jam made by a British company called Tickler. Unfortunately, Tickler manufactured the jam in only one flavor, a plum and apple mixture which grew so monotonous that when German soldiers in the trenches chanted "Gott strafe England!" ("God punish England!"), English troops chanted back, "Gott strafe Tickler!"[69]

The sameness also affected the way food was served. For the first year or so of the war, Allied soldiers in the trenches were only provided with cold foods. If there was wood in the trench, it might be possible to light a small fire and do some cooking, but as a rule there was no time, no fuel, and no opportunity to heat things up. Of course, hot foods are no more nutritious than cold ones, but hot meals can help raise body warmth in cold temperatures; moreover, many people find that heated food simply tastes better. "Warmed in a tin, Maconochie [a canned meat and vegetable mixture] was edible," remarked a British soldier. "Cold[,] it was a mankiller."[70] The complete lack of anything hot was a major cause of complaint for Allied soldiers.

But soldiers reserved their greatest scorn for food that was tasteless, spoiled, or otherwise unpleasant to eat. There was plenty of all kinds. The meat provided for soldiers, for instance, often contained enormous amounts of fat; thus, the generous-sounding meat rations permitted American soldiers were at least partly an illusion. The French used the word "fresh" to describe bread up to eight days old. Even decent food could be ruined by the circumstances. For example, it was difficult to wash dishes at the front lines. Before long, the dishes grew so encrusted with remnants of earlier meals that it was almost impossible to tell the flavor of one night's dinner from those of the previous seven.

Some of the food was downright inedible. British army biscuits were "so hard that you had to put them on a firm surface and smash them with a stone or something,"[71] reported one English private. German soldiers were sometimes given bread made from mashed turnips and sawdust, along with soup containing nettles as the vegetables. Once in a while, German troops staged raids against the Allies for the main purpose of getting palatable food.

Nonetheless, food could be a bright spot in the life of the trench warrior. Sometimes all that mattered was its presence. Food was a reminder that the purpose of a man's existence was not simply to shoot and to be shot. Mealtimes provided a chance for socializing, an opportunity to connect with other people and to take a momentary break from the horrors of the war. Food seemed to assure men that life would indeed go on. "I have never eaten finer buttered toast than in that forsaken hole in the woods,"[72] reported French soldier Marc Bloch.

Of course, the food was better appreciated if it tasted good, and sometimes it did. The soldier who nearly starved at Gallipoli had very different feelings about the food he ate upon entering the trenches for the first time. "Dinner [was]

either rice, which was good," he wrote, "or stew [made from dried meat]. . . . Later on we got fresh meat stew and steak in the mornings. This was good while it lasted."[73] Some soldiers, especially those from middle- or upper-class backgrounds, received care packages from home. Others, given short leaves, occasionally bought food from freelance vendors, nearby restaurants, or army-sponsored canteens. Though the quality of this food was not uniformly good, it tended to be better than standard army rations.

German soldiers were sometimes served bread made of mashed turnips and sawdust, causing them to stage raids against the Allies just to obtain edible food.

Water and Other Drinks

The situation with water and other drinks was much the same as the situation with food: Most soldiers did not suffer from thirst, but the quality of available drinks often left much to be desired. The water supply, in particular, was chancy. Sometimes reasonably fresh water could be trucked in from the supply lines. Other times, soldiers made do with the water that pooled in the trenches and ran into shell craters near the parapets. This water was brackish, slimy, and often polluted. When forced to drink from these holes, soldiers typically tried to strain out the excrement and the taste of chemicals; still, troops drank it when nothing else was available.

There were other drinks, too. British soldiers had their tea, Americans their coffee. By the middle of the war, many Allied soldiers carried small stoves on which these hot drinks could be prepared; others improvised

When the water supply became low, soldiers had to drink the water that pooled in shell craters. Many developed illnesses from the tainted water.

with a jam jar held over a candle. If the water was potable, then the resulting drink tasted fine. If not, then the flavoring at least might mask the odors. "Coffee," a French soldier wrote sarcastically, defining the word: "a liquid, generally blackish. . . . The cooks sometimes stir their consciences sufficiently to throw in grains of real coffee, though this is regarded as almost cheating."[74]

Alcoholic beverages were popular at the front, too. A few battalions were entirely dry; one Canadian commander replaced his troops' liquor rations with pea soup. But most soldiers had official, if limited, access to rum or brandy while on duty, and French and German troops were allowed some wine as well. Small amounts of brandy or rum were generally distributed just before soldiers were sent over the top of the trenches and into an attack. "I have had people ask me if it was true that before we went into battle we got well soaked with rum," wrote a Canadian private. "Well we got one stiff tot after struggling to reach the firing step . . . and it has very little effect on any man."[75]

Away from the trenches, many soldiers drank a great deal more alcohol. Men on leave—and to a degree those resting behind the lines as well—were often known to indulge freely in wine, beer, and anything else alcoholic they could find. But in the trenches, opportunities for serious drinking were rare. Once in a while, a support staffer assigned to pour out the rations was accused of holding some back for his own private use, and of course casks of liquor completely disappeared from time to time just as food sup-

plies did. Likewise, men who were attacking sometimes came upon whole barrels of untapped liquor, abandoned by the enemy. Still, as a general rule, drunkenness was more a problem in the rear than it was at the front.

Clothing

The trenches put all types of clothing to the test. Rain, wind, sun, and snow were all a natural part of trench life. These elements made soldiers' lives miserable. Unfortunately, the clothing the men had to wear usually did not help much. It proved almost impossible to design uniforms that would successfully withstand the punishment the clothes were subjected to. In fact, the clothes contributed to many of the illnesses the men suffered.

There was no such thing as a "standard" World War I outfit. Soldiers were typically issued a basic allowance of clothing, the exact items varying by nationality. These basics usually included jackets, socks, boots, shirts, a raincoatlike cape, and a pair of pants. This outfit was far from sufficient in cold or wet weather, however. As a result, soldiers also could have greatcoats (long, thick overcoats), fur undercoats, extra socks, and fingerless gloves.

However, some of these items were problematic in certain kinds of weather. The greatcoats, for example, were quite useful on cold, dry days, but when the rains came, they were of little help. They soaked up so much water that their weight ballooned to three times the norm, making them cumbersome and fatiguing to wear.

Similarly, although the extra pairs of dry socks helped stave off trench foot, sometimes it was virtually impossible to take the time to change out of the wet ones or to keep the feet from freezing while the change was being made.

Obtaining many of these extra items was the responsibility of the soldiers themselves. Some were able to purchase sweaters, jackets, and scarves near the front. Others brought theirs from home or had friends and relatives who could send them along. "I hope you got my letter asking for walking boots, size eight, hobnailed," wrote an English soldier to his mother. "Mark the boots 'uniform, urgent.'"[76]

But many soldiers were poor and had no money to spare for extra clothing. Their needs were only marginally met by the basic clothing allowance. Consequently, they packed their bodies in wads of newspaper, or tied rags around their hands and feet to serve as makeshift hand- and leg-warmers.

The effect was striking, as one eyewitness noted:

> [Men were] draped in canvas cloaks, like knights of old, wearing their helmet over their cap comforter and giving the appearance of some kind of ancient helm[et]. Muffled up in strange woollens sent from home, their sheepskin capes made them look like the peasant soldiers of earlier days.[77]

Sometimes the improvised clothing was effective in keeping the men warm and dry. More often, it was not. In the steady rain that fell during much of the war, poorly constructed clothing unraveled and newspapers melted away. In addition, the fabrics of the official clothing allowance did not breathe well enough in summer and let in entirely too much cold air during the winter. Even the best-made boots were constantly wet and covered with mud, thus

Bitter Winters

As luck would have it, the last two winters of the war were among the coldest in memory. The winter of 1916–1917 was probably the bitterest in northern Europe in twenty years, and the one following was no better. January and February were extremely savage, and the surrounding months were nearly as bad. Conditions were bad enough for those who could go inside, but for the men in the trenches, the situation was life-threatening.

Stories of the cold winters abound. Pools of water froze solid, and men shivered in layers of clothing. Soldiers lit small fires in the dugouts. The fires did manage to keep many of the men warm, but they let loose such acrid thick smoke that some men suffocated as they slept. The possibility of a fire raging out of control was always present, too. One man, as quoted in John Ellis's *Eye-Deep in Hell,* recalled a march in conditions that approached those of the Antarctic, "I filled my water-bottle at Mametz at midday with boiling hot tea, and when I reached Bull's Trench at 5 pm it was frozen so hard that an ordinary knife made hardly any impression on it, and we broke it instead." The bitter cold of those two winters killed many men and made life more miserable for countless others.

To escape from the harsh climate and protect themselves against enemy fire, some soldiers constructed dugouts in the trench wall.

passing on the moisture and dirt to the socks and the feet inside. "Puttees [attachments that cover the top of a boot] do not prevent mud from getting into your boots if you sink in ten inches or so," complained a British soldier. "Mackintosh [raincoat] and overcoat get saturated with mud, both inside and out."[78]

It also proved impossible to design a uniform that would repel lice. Men did what they could to fight off the menace, but nothing worked for long. Since lice congregated in the seams of clothing, soldiers could find some relief by running a candle flame along the seams. Troops had to take care, though, not to burn a hole in the clothes. The only real answer was to launder every single item of clothing, which could usually be done only when troops rotated to the rear for a few days of rest; the cycle would then begin all over again when the men returned to the fire trenches later on.

Supplies from Home

Sending extra supplies to the men at the front was not just an occasional activity engaged in when wives, mothers, and sisters had some free time. Often it was an organized and scheduled project involving entire communities. School classes banded together and collected money to buy blankets for the troops. Elderly ladies with good sewing skills gathered to sew socks, shirts, and pants for the men at the front. People at home filled sacks with various items that might possibly be of use and shipped them to random companies in the trenches. Sometimes the items were quite useful; sometimes they were quickly disposed of.

Businesses at home also got into the act. Newspapers were full of advertisements encouraging residents to buy various goods to send to troops in Belgium and France. Razors, pencils, boots, cough medicines, pipes that pointed upside down to avoid sniper fire—the list went on and on. Many of the goods for sale were purchased and sent to loved ones at war, and some of these items did brighten the days of the soldiers who received them. Others did not, being entirely too large, too impractical, or too ineffective for trench life. Regardless, stores back home often did quite well when they offered goods for shipment to the front. The combination of patriotism and capitalism was lucrative for those who took part in it.

Sleep and Shelter

Men in the trenches almost invariably suffered from sleep deprivation. "My average of sleep has been $2^1/_2$ hours in the twenty-four,"[79] wrote one soldier, and his experience was common enough among enlisted men on both sides. Sleep was difficult for several reasons. For one, nearly every minute of active frontline duty was already taken up with some assigned task or other. Another reason was the noise created by shelling and gunfire. Finally, sleep was difficult because of the conditions in the trenches. Lack of physical comfort and constant mental and emotional stress did not lend themselves to lengthy, deep, or untroubled sleep.

The shelters given to troops varied considerably according to the trenches in which they were located. Some frontline trenches had dugouts, shelters constructed in the trench's back wall. Most often these were shallow, rude scratches in the dirt, unable to provide much protection from enemy shells or the elements. "Three-quarters of an inch of candle dimly lights up a space too cramped for one man to turn round in comfortably,"[80] wrote a New Zealand officer in describing a typical dugout shared by three men.

Some dugouts, to be sure, were much more elaborate. A few had actual beds. One British dugout included tablecloths and bookshelves, and a German version had wallpaper and a gilded mirror. These luxurious accommodations were typically located in zones where successful attacks were rare. They were also almost always intended for the use of officers only. In these rooms carved into the side of the trench walls, it was nearly possible to forget that there was a war going on.

But very few of the troops benefited from this type of shelter. For most, shelter was catch-as-catch-can. The soldiers curled up in a corner of the trench, wrapped themselves in a blanket or a waterproof sheet, and slept as long as they could. They scooped out a small hole at the bottom of the mud and climbed in, hoping that they would be safe from the rats and the artillery shells for at least a few minutes. They twisted themselves into awkward shapes, using their knees as pillows. Occasionally soldiers slept well enough under these circumstances, mainly because they had reached such a level of exhaustion they could literally do almost nothing else. More common, however, was the description of this English soldier:

To lie down for two hours on a plank half sinking into a dream-ridden sleep, half hearing every noise within reach of audibility, there was little rest of body or mind. On such a bed, flesh was no protection to the bones; it was a small envelope containing a jumble of crossing nerves. Bone pressed down and wood

pressed up until the sting changed slowly into a dragging pain.[81]

While the lack of sleep presented a major problem for soldiers, the lack of any reasonable shelter presented another. There was no "indoors," no place to go to escape from the perpetual mud, rain, and ice. For the average infantryman, argued one French writer, hell meant water. Even the dugouts were not safe from the elements. "It has been raining all day," moaned a soldier, "that cold, fine, relentless winter rain against which there is no protection. . . . Water, mud. You go down in it, you slip in gently, drawn in by who knows what irresistible force."[82]

The troubles presented by the lack of adequate clothing, food, and shelter cost the lives of many men and could have destroyed many more. That it did not is a tribute to the spirit of the World War I soldier. Despite truly miserable conditions, most of the troops at the front stuck it out. They complained bitterly, they had nights when they thought they would never make it till morning, they had days when they wondered why they bothered. But in the long run they survived. They overcame hunger, thirst, cold, and exhaustion, and for better or for worse, they managed to carry out their duties as soldiers.

Chapter 5

The Brighter Side

The soldiers in the trenches had little free time, and what little time they did have for themselves was mostly spent sleeping and eating. Life at the front was deadly serious business, so there was not much opportunity for play. Nevertheless, to do effective work, the men needed to take some time away from the constant worries about weather, shells, and disease and devote themselves to recreation and entertainment.

Recreation was mainly available when regiments rotated out of the trenches. In the English army, "rest" periods away from the front meant morning drills and practices, followed by sports in the afternoon and formal entertainment in the evenings. Soccer was quite popular among the troops, but shooting and riding competitions were common too. Though free time was rare, few men seem to have resented the lack of it. Instead, most soldiers were delighted to take part in the games, and soccer balls were among the most prized possessions of any regiment.

During the evenings, troops occasionally attended performances known as divisional concerts or divisional follies. These were staged productions set up and performed by the soldiers themselves. For the most part, these performances consisted of a vaudeville-like mix of songs, dances, and comedy routines. Many of the pieces would have been indistinguishable from numbers in a similar show performed at home. The soldiers sang popular songs of the era and based their comedy on jokes familiar to any audience that knew the culture. But just as often, the performances drew heavily on military themes, as in this satirical performance seen by a British army physician behind the lines in 1917:

> During our last tour [of duty] I went to a Show. It is a kind of Divisional Follies, but none the less good for that [that is, quite good anyhow]. . . all done by men

who have been over the Top [taken part in a charge; actual soldiers], or at least done front line work. . . . The plot is laid in 1967, and is really awfully clever. War still progressing, and the men's grandsons were rolling up. Leave only granted once in twenty-one years.[83]

Army officials also brought in talented professional performers to entertain the troops. Perhaps the biggest name among the singers and actors who came to France was a Scottish singer and comedian named Harry Lauder, whose only son had been killed on the front lines midway through the war. Movies were in their infancy, too, and many troops spent their evenings watching popular films of the time. Charlie Chaplin, newly arrived on the cinematic scene, was a special favorite of many of the troops.

During the limited recreation time available to soldiers, most enjoyed playing soccer or competing in shooting and riding competitions.

Games

Even in the trenches, it was possible to have fun once in a while, and soldiers seized every chance to do so. Not surprisingly, recreation was easier to manage in some places than in others. In particular, it was easier to have fun in reserve and supply trenches than it was closer to the neutral zone. Not only were the forward trenches closer to the fighting, but life in the rear zones was more predictable; it was rare to be unexpectedly summoned to go over the top, take part in a raid, or take on sentry duty for a wounded comrade.

Recreation was also simpler in stretches of the line where the fighting was irregular. In some places and at some times, fighting did dwindle to virtually nothing as the two sides adopted a so-called live-and-let-live philosophy. In such cases, the gentleman's agreement that said there would be no shelling during breakfast was expanded to include nearly the entire day, and soldiers moved about more or less at will on their own side. Low-ranking commanders sometimes turned a blind eye to this strategy, but higher-ranking officers had different ideas. "Don't let anything show itself on the other side [of the Marne River] and live,"[84] directed a newly arrived leader to Allied troops accustomed to the live-and-let-live philosophy.

When they could spare time and space, troops on both sides loved playing games. Card games were especially popular, and men played in all conditions: while at rest, while in support trenches, and even within

Soldier Slang

The soldiers in the trenches soon developed their own slang terms for objects and responsibilities. A few of these terms became so well-known that they slipped into ordinary vocabulary, and others gained continued use in the military. However, most were left on the battlefield. These are some typical soldier terms originated or popularized by the British and American armies:

Boche, Fritz, Jerry: German soldier.
Big Bertha: The name given to a certain type of German artillery gun, jokingly named in honor of Bertha Krupp von Bohlen und Halback, who owned the factory at which the guns were made.
chow: Food.
doughboy: American soldier.
get it: To be killed.
zero hour: The time at which an attack was to begin.
Holy Joe: An army chaplain.
egg: A hand grenade or a bomb.
rookie: A new recruit, a soldier who had just arrived at the front.
smoke screen: Billows of smoke caused by artillery fire and intended to shield advancing troops.
foxhole: A small ditch for three or four men.
trench coat: A fashionable coat worn by some British officers at the front.

sight of the barbed wire if time and physical health allowed. "What puzzles me is just how little sleep these card players can exist on," wrote a British private. "They play cards . . . whenever they have a minute off duty, snatching an occasional hour of sleep at odd times."[85]

It was possible to find almost any kind of card game going on within a trench as long as the shooting was not too fierce. One well-known British card game of the time was a form of blackjack known as brag and bank. Another popular game among the English troops was a version of bingo, which was called "house" by those who played it. The German army favored a three-player game called skat, and the French played a variety of games as well.

As might have been expected, most of these games involved gambling. Soldiers bet on practically anything. Americans played craps, a dice game that sometimes threatened to completely take over the attention of the troops. German troops bet heavily on a game called Wattepusten, which involved placing bets on a player's ability to blow tufts of cotton at targets. "If [gambling] is as widespread as these young men admit," wrote an observer astonished by the amount of gambling in the Allied armies, "I'm not sure but that wine and women are less serious evils."[86]

The possibility of getting something for nothing was part of the fun of gambling, but soldiers also acted out the reality of their lives when they gambled. The fact was that life in the trenches was a form of gambling. Every day, shells whizzed down from the sky; shots rang out from unseen snipers. Some hit their targets, while others missed. The soldiers who survived were quite lucky, and most knew it, but some began to think of themselves as almost invincible. Their luck, they believed, would surely hold out; moreover, it would apply to gambling games as well as to avoiding death.

Music

Singing was another favorite activity among the soldiers in the trenches. Cards and dice used little space; singing required none at all. It was not necessary for there to be a cease-fire or a quiet set of trenches for men to sing; indeed, singing could be done even while soldiers worked. Better yet, music often kept the men's hopes up and helped them deal with the stress of being at the front.

Soldier songs were many. Some men preferred to sing current songs popular at home, while others enjoyed familiar folk songs. The lyrics of most of these songs had little or nothing to do with the war effort. Still, they reminded the men of home, and in some small way they helped to bring the singers and listeners closer to those they loved. "When you're a long, long way from home," one English song ran, "your mother's voice rings in your ears."[87] Songs such as this one made the men at the front think of their own wives, sweethearts, and mothers, and connected them more closely to those across the sea.

The lyrical connections were not only with the home front. Soldiers soon began associating certain songs with the war and with one another. The strains of a particular ballad could remind soldiers of a friend who had died in a raid or been wounded in a shelling. "The cheap popular songs of the last few years can move me infinitely more than the divinest music," wrote a well-educated English soldier, "because of the men I have heard sing them."[88] Some songs thus became connected with the war in the minds of the men who served at the front.

Indeed, popular music made a strong impression on men in the trenches. Some men noted that the rhythmic reports of machine guns being fired matched the beat of songs popular back home. One man found himself singing a tune called "Policeman's Holiday" in time to the sounds of the war. "A quaint idea," he wrote, "to think you might 'go out' to a senseless catch-tune played on a lethal weapon!"[89]

During lulls in the fighting, many soldiers relaxed by playing cards or gambling. Pictured are Russian soldiers playing cards.

A few songs came to be widely associated with the war in the public mind, too, although the songs originally had no connection with it. English soldiers, for instance, loved to sing "It's a Long Way to Tipperary," a song actually written several years before the war broke out. The words of the song, which tell the story of an Irishman far away from his home town of Tipperary who longs to return, struck a chord with servicemen. Mired in French or Belgian mud and dodging artillery explosions at every turn, they found themselves longing for their own English homeland. Ever since, the song has been thought of not simply as a song of the period but as a song specifically connected with the war.

Likewise, patriotic songs were often sung among the troops in the trenches. These songs helped remind the men of the home and country for which they fought, and the people they were risking death to protect. While many songs written by composers at home were disparaged or ignored by the troops, George M. Cohan's "Over There" was one example of an extremely popular song both at home and in the front lines. In short, snappy lines, the song promised that American troops would head to France to help the Allies:

Over there
Over there
Send the word
Send the word
Over there

That the boys are coming
The boys are coming
The drums rum-tuming everywhere.[90]

Live and Let Live

In some sections along the western front, soldiers at times adopted a live-and-let-live attitude. They shot only enough to keep commanders happy, and otherwise went about their daily business with an unspoken agreement that the other side would not take advantage of lapses in judgment. One British soldier recalled a month during which there were no casualties at all in his unit. Another remembered a stretch of time when soldiers from both sides walked on the parapets during the daytime without fear of being hit. There was even a case in which soldiers were forbidden to shoot at game birds in no-man's-land for fear that they might hit an enemy soldier.

Some historians have concluded from these stories that the live-and-let-live philosophy was prevalent along the line. From this distance, it is impossible to know for sure how widespread the practice was. Since high-ranking commanders disapproved, much of the inactivity was unofficial; few people wrote about it at the time or called attention to it. As a result, it is certainly possible that many more troops had an easy time of it than the records indicate.

However, occurrences of live and let live seem to have been fairly rare, limited to a relatively few places during relatively short periods of times. The carnage in the trenches was too great for truces to have been truly common. Too many soldiers in the trenches were wounded or killed by fighting; too many were psychologically damaged; too many came home with horrible recollections of dead and dying friends. A widespread philosophy of live and let live would not have produced such results.

All combatants had several nationalistic songs like "Over There." The German song "The Watch on the Rhine," for instance, served a similar purpose.

But many of the most popular soldier songs were not at all well-known at home until after the war was over. Like the satiric sketches in the divisional follies away from the front, these songs expressed quite clearly what it was like to be a soldier. A few spoke movingly of the sorrows, fears, and loneliness of soldier life. More, however, were humorous. Many soldier songs poked fun at the local inhabitants, as did this British and American jibe at the French women:

Many soldiers turned to music for solace and motivation. A favorite song that was sung by Allied soldiers was George M. Cohan's "Over There," a song promising help to America's allies.

Mademoiselle from Armentieres, parlay-vous?
Mademoiselle from Armentieres, parlay-vous?
Mademoiselle from Armentieres,
She hadn't been kissed in forty years,
Hinky, dinky, parlay-vous. [91]

Others made light of death, wounds, or disease. As British soldiers sang:

If you want to find the old battalion,
I know where they are . . .
I've seen 'em,
I've seen 'em,
Hanging on the old barbed wire. [92]

While singing was the easiest method of making music in the trenches, a few soldiers did have small musical instruments as part of their personal belongings. Harmonicas, often called mouth organs by the troops, were particularly popular. They were small enough to slip into a pocket, and they could easily be held in one hand. Those who did not own harmonicas brought along penny whistles or mouth harps, or they blew through tissue paper held up to the teeth of combs. A few officers had gramophones, early versions of record players, and the rear trenches were sometimes filled with the strains of classical music from recordings played on these machines.

Reading and Writing

As might be expected, the trenches were not good places for reading. For many troops, that did not create a problem; they were illiterate anyway. Some soldiers, however, did bring books to the front. Most literate soldiers, though, confined their reading to the rear trenches or—better yet—to the rest areas behind the lines. Men's tastes in literature varied, but it is safe to say that the men who did pack books carried either the Bible or current fiction of the period. Very few men seem to have spent much time reading serious literature in the forward trenches.

Even if the reading of books was uncommon at the front, reading of other material was much more in evidence. Perhaps the most popular type of reading matter was the letter. Any soldier who could do so kept up a correspondence with loved ones at home. Postal authorities were swamped; the British system alone delivered 12.5 million letters a week to the front during most of 1918. Unless there was a battle raging, the men in the lines received their mail with the utmost speed. The letters arrived on a daily basis, brought from the rear trenches by supply troops.

Men loved receiving letters from family and friends. "Out here news of home is like food and drink to us, however trivial," wrote one English soldier. "Indeed, this life is like a dream and the old life is the only reality. We live on memories." [93] Letters were so important that men who did not receive mail often asked to borrow letters mailed to friends. It did not matter whether the borrower knew the letter writer or not; simply having a letter, any letter, meant a great deal to the men in the trenches.

Not only did the men read letters, they wrote them, too. On both sides, these letters were subject to censorship; just as with the newspapers, it would not do for men to give away too much information in case the letters fell into enemy hands. Many soldiers also censored themselves, preferring not to tell the truth about the war as they saw and experienced it. "[Our] correspondence

[was] full of convenient lies," wrote one soldier. "We described *their* war to them, which satisfied them[,] and we kept ours a secret."[94] These letters were often characterized by a breeziness the writer did not feel, or simply reported that all was well without going into the grim details. Other letters, however, were carefully thought-out documents detailing the writer's state of mind.

Regardless of the letters' content, most men eagerly wrote as many letters as they could. Throughout the trenches, even in the fire trench during slack periods, men could be seen hunched over a rock or a sandbag, scrawling a few lines to a mother, a sister, or a friend. Many of these letters still survive. Some soldiers preferred to send postcards, which could be purchased from supply stores near the front lines. Even those who could not write often asked friends to do it for them.

Newspapers

Newspapers were another source of reading matter. At the beginning of the war, in particular, many soldiers eagerly scrutinized commercial newspapers, hoping for information about the war and its progress. Unfortunately, censorship usually won out over accurate reporting. Army officials were reluctant to allow any information about the war to be printed. Locations of trenches, expected troop movements, potential plans of generals—all were off limits. As a result, the newspapers most often offered troops a bland and useless series of feature articles, interspersed with vague and misleading references to the war. Not surprisingly, soldiers

Friends

World War I took place during a time of improving communication and transportation. It was not at all unusual for soldiers from one country to have visited an enemy nation before the war. Sometimes they even had connections in the other country. Some Germans, for instance, had relatives who had emigrated to Britain or the United States before hostilities broke out. College-educated German soldiers, in turn, often knew Allied soldiers who had come to one of Germany's universities to study. In extreme cases, soldiers found themselves on the field opposite a man they actually had known, as in this story told by a Canadian lieutenant, quoted in *War Letters of Fallen Englishmen:*

A bird cage [that is, a sniper's outpost] facing us in Sanctuary Wood was at regular intervals occupied by an expert sniper who had served with one of our number as a waiter in Broadway, New York. His cage was only about twenty yards away. He killed one or two of us every day. In the intervals he engaged with us in racy conversation.

Not all men responded the same way as this sniper did. Later in the same letter, the lieutenant described how a friend of his had been spotted by a different German sharpshooter. As it turned out, "my friend was in the hands of . . . an Oxford graduate," the lieutenant explained, "a man who—despite repeated requests not to be used on the British Front—had been sent against us." Clearly, he had decided not to shoot at any British soldiers; rather than fire at the easy target, the sniper told the terrified Englishman about his British connections and allowed him to go.

soon stopped reading these papers altogether.

But standard newspapers were not the only news sources available to troops. Many army divisions supported newspapers of their own. Some of these were more or less official mouthpieces of the military; they were staffed by professional writers and produced at a good distance from the front. Others, however, were much less polished—and much more genuinely the work of the ordinary soldiers. Closer to what might be called a newsletter today, these papers varied in size, thickness, and print quality. They did have one thing in common, however. As one French paper boasted, "Le Crocodile is . . . written, laid out and produced at the front. . . . This issue is printed in an underground shelter 1400 meters from the Boches [Germans]."[95]

No one knows how many of these newspapers were actually in business during the

Literate soldiers eagerly read newspapers and letters from home to feel a connection with the outside world.

war, but the French army alone had at least several hundred. Most produced only a handful of copies and distributed them only on a very small scale. One editor bragged that his paper's circulation had risen to three hundred for each issue. Self-appointed editors and reporters wrote what pleased them and used primitive materials, such as gelatin mix, to create grainy copies of their work.

Often, the main thrust of these articles involved morale and entertainment. "Our ambition is simply to entertain you for a moment," explained one editor, "and if we manage even for an instant to bring you pleasure, we will only be too happy to have achieved our aim."[96] But these papers also wrote more specifically about the war itself: about the dangers of being a soldier, about the feelings of homesickness and depression that affected so many men, and about the patriotic sentiment important to many of the troops. A few papers were also openly scornful of military policy, at least until army officials found out what was going on.

Companionship

Perhaps the most common form of recreation, however, was cheap and easy: It was companionship. In the front lines, men of very different backgrounds were thrown together for hours and days at a time. Their lives depended on one another. The stresses of trench warfare quickly united the men and created bonds that did not easily break. Talk, laughter, and sharing the same experiences all led to stronger connections among

Class Lines

The war threw together men of very different backgrounds. Often, the strongest connections between men fell along socioeconomic lines; peasants, small-business owners, and the gentry tended to feel most comfortable around others of their own kind. Sometimes, however, connections were made across class divisions, as scholar Marc Bloch describes in his *Memoirs of War, 1914–15*:

> Of all my comrades who fell . . . there is none I mourned more than F., who was the sergeant of my second half platoon. F.'s line of work was not one usually considered important. . . . He had scant education and could barely read. Yet no one has done more to make me understand the beauty of a truly noble and sensitive soul. . . . He devoted himself to making life more agreeable for those of his men he thought were poor, and shared with them those small treats that are beyond price in the field. . . . Unquestionably his main desire and his greatest effort was to ensure that his half platoon should "get along well together." When I lost him, I lost a moral support.

the men—and served as a vital way of passing the time.

Except during the worst of attacks, conversation was nearly constant in the trenches. Men spoke together for all kinds of reasons. One was to relieve boredom. Many of the duties at the front could be extremely monotonous, and the men assigned to them found they went faster with a friend. Another was to relieve fear. Just as men sang humorous songs about disaster to make it seem less real, so too did they laugh and joke together about things hard to face alone.

But perhaps most of all, they talked because doing so made them feel more fully human. Under the miserable conditions at the front, it was easy to feel like a target, a thing rather than a person. To reach out to another breathing, feeling creature could make the experience almost bearable. Some men discovered, much to their surprise, that class and geographic distinctions diminished in the trenches. "He sings dirty songs and swears," wrote one upper-class English soldier about the typical soldier he had encountered at the front, "but get to know him, start by loving him, believe in him through thick and thin, and you will not go unrewarded."[97]

The ties between the men were strong indeed. "My whole being is bound up with my men, heart, body, and soul," wrote a soldier whose will distributed his possessions among the men of his battalion. "Nothing else seems to matter."[98] Typically, small groups of close friends would form in each fighting unit, the number varying anywhere from two or three up to a dozen or so. These men would look out for each other; they would relieve one another on duty when they could, share their meager possessions, write the inevitable letter home after a friend's death.

While there was an automatic connection between any two men who served on the same side during the war, the basic building block was this small group of friends. To some soldiers, the lives of these friends soon became nearly as important as their own lives. In *All Quiet on the Western Front*, for instance, the deep and abiding connections among a group of friends in the German army are described. "It is impossible," writes the narrator when his good friend Stanislaus Katczinsky is severely wounded, "that my friend Kat—Kat with the drooping shoulders and the poor, thin moustache, Kat, whom I know as I know no other man, Kat with whom I have shared these years—it is impossible that perhaps I shall not see Kat again."[99]

Across the Lines

Occasionally, there was even a feeling of companionship between the men on opposite sides of the war. More than once, troops declared an unofficial cease-fire when men on the other side seemed to need it. After one particularly bloody battle, for instance, an English minister came to France to search for his son, missing and presumed dead. He spent quite some time looking through the neutral zone for the young man. During that time, no German shot at him. On other occasions, men on both sides chose to allow enemies trapped in the neutral zone a clear path to freedom.

Basic humanity prompted other communications back and forth. "The Germans were quite nice two days ago," wrote an English soldier, describing an incident in which German troops had shot at three of his comrades in the neutral zone and had taken two of them prisoner. "In the morning they put up a notice in German: 'Tho' alive when we took him into our trench, No. 1238 Pte. [private] Summers has since died from wounds.'"[100] The Allies responded in kind, writing a notice which said, "Danke sehr" ("Many thanks" in German).

Less common were moments when soldiers in opposite trenches swarmed into the neutral zone to swap stories, souvenirs, and more. In some cases the two sides even visited each other's fortifications. The most famous of these brief truces occurred on Christmas Day, 1914, when Germans at one spot along the line met with English troops in no-man's-land. "Scots and Huns [Germans] were fraternizing in the most genuine possible manner," wrote an English commander. "Every sort of souvenir was exchanged, addresses given and received, photos of families shown."[101] Later, the two sides sang their favorite songs for each other. The day ended when the Germans invited the English into their trenches for a special dinner. On other similar occasions, the men played soccer, boxed, or prayed together in the neutral zone.

A Glimmer of Light

Despite the horrors of life in the trenches, some soldiers did manage to find signs of good in the world around them. The truth was that even the worst days did have a glimmer of light. Sometimes that glimmer was the friendship extended by a fellow soldier or even a kindhearted enemy. Sometimes it was nothing more than the fact of personal survival after a day's heavy shelling, or the receiving of a letter or two from loved ones.

Even the battlefield itself had its own form of beauty, remarked upon by many soldiers. "It is wonderful going out into 'No Man's Land,'" wrote a British soldier. "Stars and wet grass, and nothing between you and the enemy, and every now and then a very soft and beautiful blue-white light from a Very pistol."[102] The place was one of terrible danger, and the blue-white light a signal that death could come at any moment, and yet this soldier used the words "beautiful" and "wonderful" to describe the place and the experience.

He was not alone. Many men marveled at the life which stubbornly refused to leave even the most burned-out neutral zones. No-man's-land contained flowering bushes, vegetables, and other kinds of plant life. Rabbits and pheasants found ways of surviving in and around shell holes. So did songbirds. "It was the first decent thing we had heard for a long time," one man wrote about hearing a nightingale sing. "There was something infinitely sweet and sad about it, as if the countryside were singing gently to itself."[103]

But as this soldier implied, the bird songs and the other signs of life and beauty were not all positive. To be sure, they gave soldiers hope, assuring them that there were far greater things in life than trench warfare. Yet they also served as a bitter reminder that all was not as it should have been. For many soldiers, the presence of this beauty and life among all the death and terror seemed nothing more than a mocking irony. This irony is readily apparent in the first stanza of

Canadian poet John MCrae's "In Flanders Fields," perhaps the best-known poem to come out of the Great War:

> In Flanders fields the poppies blow
> Between the crosses, row on row,
> That mark our place, and in the sky,
> The larks, still bravely singing, fly,
> Scarce heard amid the guns below. [104]

There is no doubt that death and disaster were far more common in the trenches than any sign of beauty. Most soldiers, it is safe to say, scarcely noticed any good in their experience at the front, at least not until they reflected back on it many months or years later. In this view, the poppies and the larks of McRae's poem were only an illusion. Like all recreational opportunities in the trenches, the occasional beauty of the surroundings paled in comparison to the reality of life at the front.

Canadian poet John MCrae's poem "In Flanders Fields" celebrates the triumph of the human spirit in the midst of tragedy and death.

And yet the beauty, the friendships, the fun did carry enormous importance. They were a reminder that there was more to life than dodging bullets and hoping against hope that the next shell would fail to explode, more to life than cold and wet and rain and mud. They were a way of finding meaning even under the worst conditions that most soldiers could imagine. The death of a friend unleashed emotions in men which many did not know they had. The song of a lark could do the same. The games, the music, the letters, the swapping of stories across no-man's-land—in all these ways, soldiers demonstrated their refusal to give in to the horrors of the war. The horrors were powerful, but perhaps the strength of the human spirit was more powerful still.

★ Notes ★

Introduction: Into the Earth

1. Quoted in Denis Winter, *Death's Men*. New York: Penguin Books, 1978, p. 80.

Chapter 1: Fighting

2. Quoted in John Ellis, *Eye-Deep in Hell: Trench Warfare in World War I*. Baltimore, MD: Johns Hopkins University Press, 1976, p. 33.
3. Winter, *Death's Men*, p. 82.
4. Quoted in Ellis, *Eye-Deep in Hell*, p. 78.
5. Quoted in Laurence Housman, ed., *War Letters of Fallen Englishmen*. London: Victor Gollancz, 1930, pp. 119–20.
6. Quoted in Ellis, *Eye-Deep in Hell*, p. 68.
7. Quoted in Ellis, *Eye-Deep in Hell*, p. 89.
8. Quoted in Housman, *War Letters of Fallen Englishmen*, p. 171.
9. Quoted in Ellis, *Eye-Deep in Hell*, p. 63.
10. Quoted in Housman, *War Letters of Fallen Englishmen*, p. 90.
11. Quoted in Winter, *Death's Men*, p. 123.
12. Quoted in Stephane Audoin-Rouzeau, *Men at War 1914–1918*. Oxford, England: Berg, 1992, p. 72.
13. Quoted in John Terraine, *The Great War 1914–1918: A Pictorial History*. Garden City, NY: Doubleday, 1965, p. 135.
14. Quoted in Winter, *Death's Men*, p. 124.
15. Quoted in Winter, *Death's Men*, p. 93.
16. Quoted in Winter, *Death's Men*, p. 92.
17. Boyd Cable, *Between the Lines*. New York: E. P. Dutton, 1915, pp. 126–27.
18. Quoted in Winter, *Death's Men*, p. 178.
19. Quoted in Terraine, *The Great War 1914–1918*, p. 246.
20. Quoted in Ellis, *Eye-Deep in Hell*, p. 93.
21. Quoted in Winter, *Death's Men*, p. 214.

Chapter 2: Duties and Discipline

22. Quoted in Housman, *War Letters of Fallen Englishmen*, p. 282.
23. Quoted in Ellis, *Eye-Deep in Hell*, p. 29.
24. Quoted in Winter, *Death's Men*, p. 83.
25. Quoted in Winter, *Death's Men*, p. 85.
26. Quoted in Ellis, *Eye-Deep in Hell*, p. 38
27. Quoted in Housman, *War Letters of Fallen Englishmen*, pp. 88–89.
28. Quoted in Winter, *Death's Men*, p. 85.
29. Marc Bloch, *Memoirs of War, 1914–15*. Ithaca, NY: Cornell University Press, 1980, p. 152.
30. Quoted in Audoin-Rouzeau, *Men at War 1914–1918*, pp. 38–39.
31. Quoted in Ellis, *Eye-Deep in Hell*, p. 75.
32. J. M. Winter, *The Experience of World War I*. New York: Oxford University Press, 1989, p. 158.
33. Quoted in Ellis, *Eye-Deep in Hell*, p. 181.
34. Quoted in Ellis, *Eye-Deep in Hell*, p. 188.

35. Quoted in Laurence Stallings, *The Doughboys: The Story of the AEF 1917–1918.* New York: Harper and Row, 1963, p. 21.

36. Quoted in Reginald Pound, *The Lost Generation.* London: Constable, 1964, p. 112.

37. Quoted in Ellis, *Eye-Deep in Hell,* p. 98.

Chapter 3: Injury, Illness, and Death

38. Quoted in Terraine, *The Great War 1914–1918,* p. 264.

39. Quoted in Winter, *Death's Men,* p. 186.

40. Quoted in Audoin-Rouzeau, *Men at War 1914–1918,* p. 78.

41. Quoted in Winter, *Death's Men,* p. 203.

42. Quoted in Housman, *War Letters of Fallen Englishmen,* p. 171.

43. Quoted in Housman, *War Letters of Fallen Englishmen,* p. 117.

44. Quoted in Ellis, *Eye-Deep in Hell,* p. 175.

45. Quoted in Winter, *Death's Men,* p. 194.

46. Quoted in Ellis, *Eye-Deep in Hell,* p. 109.

47. Quoted in Winter, *Death's Men,* p. 198.

48. Erich Maria Remarque, *All Quiet on the Western Front.* Boston: Little, Brown, 1929, p. 49.

49. Quoted in Ellis, *Eye-Deep in Hell,* p. 54.

50. Quoted in Housman, *War Letters of Fallen Englishmen,* p. 92.

51. Quoted in Housman, *War Letters of Fallen Englishmen,* p. 118.

52. Quoted in Housman, *War Letters of Fallen Englishmen,* p. 301.

53. John Oxenham, *High Altars.* New York: George H. Doran, 1918, p. 9.

54. Quoted in Housman, *War Letters of Fallen Englishmen,* p. 123.

55. Quoted in Terraine, *The Great War 1914–1918,* p. 264.

56. Quoted in Winter, *Death's Men,* p. 208.

57. Quoted in Audoin-Rouzeau, *Men at War 1914–1918,* p. 82.

58. Quoted in Pound, *The Lost Generation,* p. 257.

59. Quoted in Winter, *Death's Men,* p. 118.

60. Quoted in Audoin-Rouzeau, *Men at War 1914–1918,* p. 54.

61. Quoted in Ellis, *Eye-Deep in Hell,* pp. 119–21.

62. Winter, *Death's Men,* p. 140.

Chapter 4: Supplies and Survival

63. Oxenham, *High Altars,* p. 55.

64. Quoted in Winter, *The Experience of World War I,* p. 135.

65. Quoted in Oxenham, *High Altars,* p. 56.

66. Oxenham, *High Altars,* p. 54.

67. Quoted in Housman, *War Letters of Fallen Englishmen,* p. 93.

68. Quoted in Audoin-Rouzeau, *Men at War 1914–1918,* p. 60.

69. Quoted in Winter, *Death's Men,* p. 234.

70. Quoted in Ellis, *Eye-Deep in Hell,* p. 129.

71. Quoted in Ellis, *Eye-Deep in Hell,* p. 129.

72. Bloch, *Memoirs of War, 1914–15,* p. 135.

73. Quoted in Housman, *War Letters of Fallen Englishmen,* p. 93.

74. Quoted in Audoin-Rouzeau, *Men at War 1914–1918,* p. 43.

75. Quoted in Ellis, *Eye-Deep in Hell,* p. 96.

76. Quoted in Housman, *War Letters of Fallen Englishmen,* pp. 212–13.

77. Quoted in Ellis, *Eye-Deep in Hell,* p. 52.

78. Quoted in Winter, *Death's Men,* p. 96.

79. Quoted in Housman, *War Letters of Fallen Englishmen*, p. 282.

80. Quoted in Ellis, *Eye-Deep in Hell*, p. 17.

81. Quoted in Winter, *Death's Men*, p. 100.

82. Quoted in Audoin-Rouzeau, *Men at War 1914–1918*, p. 38.

Chapter 5: The Brighter Side

83. Quoted in Ellis, *Eye-Deep in Hell*, p. 145.

84. Quoted in John S. D. Eisenhower, *Yanks: The Epic Story of the American Army in World War I*. New York: Free Press, 2001, p. 157.

85. Quoted in Ellis, *Eye-Deep in Hell*, p. 148.

86. Quoted in Ellis, *Eye-Deep in Hell*, p. 151.

87. Quoted in Winter, *Death's Men*, p. 163.

88. Quoted in Housman, *War Letters of Fallen Englishmen*, p. 239.

89. Quoted in Housman, *War Letters of Fallen Englishmen*, p. 210.

90. Quoted in Winter, *The Experience of World War I*, p. 128.

91. Quoted in John A. and Alan Lomax, *Best Loved American Folk Songs*. New York: Grosset and Dunlap, 1947, p. 122.

92. Quoted in Winter, *The Experience of World War I*, p. 128.

93. Quoted in Winter, *Death's Men*, p. 165.

94. Quoted in Ellis, *Eye-Deep in Hell*, p. 139.

95. Quoted in Audoin-Rouzeau, *Men at War 1914–1918*, p. 4.

96. Quoted in Audoin-Rouzeau, *Men at War 1914–1918*, p. 12.

97. Quoted in Housman, *War Letters of Fallen Englishmen*, p. 239.

98. Quoted in Ellis, *Eye-Deep in Hell*, p. 200.

99. Remarque, *All Quiet on the Western Front*, pp. 243–44.

100. Quoted in Housman, *War Letters of Fallen Englishmen*, p. 172.

101. Quoted in Housman, *War Letters of Fallen Englishmen*, p. 146.

102. Quoted in Housman, *War Letters of Fallen Englishmen*, p. 301.

103. Quoted in Winter, *Death's Men*, p. 105.

104. Quoted in J. W. Cunliffe, ed., *Poems of the Great War*. New York: Macmillan, 1917, p. 180.

★ For Further Reading ★

Jonathan Gawne, *Over There! The American Soldier in World War I*. Philadelphia, PA: Chelsea House, 1999. Though the emphasis is on American soldiers during the war, there is some information on the Europeans in trenches as well.

Kathlyn and Martin K. Gay, *World War I*. New York: Twenty-First Century Books, 1995. A short, readable account of the war in all its forms.

Zachary Kent, *World War I: The War to End All Wars*. Hillside, NJ: Enslow, 1994. A well-written general history of the war; includes several pages and some good quotes regarding the trench system and life at the front.

Donald Sommerville, *World War I*. Austin, TX: Raintree/Steck Vaughn, 1999. A general history with some information on battles and life at the front.

✫ Works Consulted ✫

Stephane Audoin-Rouzeau, *Men at War 1914–1918*. Oxford, England: Berg, 1992. A scholarly discussion of the trench newspapers in France, including how they were produced, who the editors were, and why they were put into circulation; it also quotes extensively from surviving issues.

Marc Bloch, *Memoirs of War, 1914–15*. Ithaca, NY: Cornell University Press, 1980. Later known as a teacher and historian, Bloch served as an officer in a French regiment. The memoirs were written during the war while Bloch was on sick leave; they tell only some of his experiences.

Boyd Cable, *Between the Lines*. New York: E. P. Dutton, 1915. Cable was a British journalist. His book, written near the front very early in the war, tried to explain the circumstances of trench warfare to the average person at home.

J. W. Cunliffe, ed., *Poems of the Great War*. New York: Macmillan, 1917. A compilation of poems—good, bad, and indifferent—produced during the early years of the war by professional writers and soldiers alike.

Edward Arthur Dolph, *Sound Off! Soldier Songs from the Revolution to World War II*. New York: Farrar and Rinehart, 1942. An entertaining and instructive book of American war songs through the ages. Includes a long chapter on the music of World War I.

John S. D. Eisenhower, *Yanks: The Epic Story of the American Army in World War I*. New York: Free Press, 2001. A thorough and detailed study of American soldiers in the war. Also includes information on the building of the army and the deployment of the troops.

John Ellis, *Eye-Deep in Hell: Trench Warfare in World War I*. Baltimore, MD: Johns Hopkins University Press, 1976. A well-organized and carefully detailed book about trench warfare in all its forms. Several chapters specifically cover daily life, while others discuss weaponry, attitudes of soldiers, and more.

Stuart Berg Flexner, *I Hear America Talking*. New York: Van Nostrand, 1976. A book of word and phrase origins, including slang terms from different periods in American history; has a useful section on some of the words used by World War I soldiers.

Philip Gibbs, *From Bapaume to Passchendaele, 1917*. London: William Heinemann, 1918. A long and detailed account of the war adventures of several English regiments.

Laurence Housman, ed., *War Letters of Fallen Englishmen*. London: Victor Gollancz, 1930. A moving and valuable collection of letters written at the front by British soldiers who later were killed in the war. These letters have the advantage of immediacy; the emotions and ideas they express were very much on the men's minds as they wrote.

John A. and Alan Lomax, *Best Loved American Folk Songs*. New York: Grosset and Dunlap, 1947. A collection of traditional songs, including several from World War I.

John Oxenham, *High Altars*. New York: George H. Doran, 1918. A short book written by an Englishman who visited the trenches. The book is valuable today principally as an example of wartime propaganda: Oxenham's picture of the German army is consistently evil, his vision of the Allies unfailingly positive.

Reginald Pound, *The Lost Generation*. London: Constable, 1964. The title refers to the great numbers of Englishmen who were born during the 1890s and killed in the war. Pound specifically tells the story of men from the upper classes of society who enlisted and often did not come back.

Erich Maria Remarque, *All Quiet on the Western Front*. Boston: Little, Brown, 1929. Perhaps the greatest novel to come out of the war. Remarque served in the German army and fictionalized many of his own experiences in writing the book; it has always been considered a great anti-war novel.

Keith Robbins, *The First World War*. Oxford, England: Oxford University Press, 1984. A short but thorough history of the war, including some information on trench conditions.

Laurence Stallings, *The Doughboys: The Story of the AEF 1917–1918*. New York: Harper and Row, 1963. A breezy narrative of the American troops and their role in the conflict.

John Terraine, *The Great War 1914–1918: A Pictorial History*. Garden City, NY: Doubleday, 1965. An excellent source of background information, well illustrated and organized by date, forming a clear narrative of battles and the slow Allied march to victory.

Denis Winter, *Death's Men*. New York: Penguin Books, 1978. A thoughtful and well-written study of World War I English soldiers: their hopes, their disappointments, their lives. Includes much information on the trenches and on the men's reactions to the conditions around them.

J. M. Winter, *The Experience of World War I*. New York: Oxford University Press, 1989. A well-illustrated book covering all aspects of the conflict: political, cultural, social, and more.

☆ Index ☆

★ Picture Credits ★

☆ About the Author ☆

Stephen Currie is the author of more than forty books and many magazine articles. Among his nonfiction titles are *Music in the Civil War, Birthday a Day, Problem Play, We Have Marched Together: The Working Children's Crusade,* and *Life in a Wild West Show.* He is also a first- and second-grade teacher. He lives in upstate New York with his wife, Amity, and two children, Irene and Nicholas.